GET OUTTA
MY FACE!

GET OUTTA
MY FACE!

HOW TO REACH ANGRY, UNMOTIVATED TEENS
WITH BIBLICAL COUNSEL

RICK HORNE

Shepherd Press
Wapwallopen, Pennsylvania

Get Outta My Face!
©2009 by Richard Horne

ISBN: 978-0-9815400-7-8

   All inquiries should be addressed to: Shepherd Press, P.O. Box 24, Wapwallopen, PA 18660.

Page design and typesetting by Lakeside Design Plus
Cover design by Tobias' Outerwear for Books

First Printing, 2009
Printed in the United States of America

RRD   19   18   17   16   15   14   13   12   11   10   09
13   12   11   10   9   8   7   6   5   4   3

To my two sons, four daughters, and hundreds of teens who constantly teach me that God has placed them in my life to respect them, love them, and serve them with the richness of the Gospel first, and any other way I am able.

CONTENTS

ACKNOWLEDGMENTS

If there is any wisdom, insight, discernment, or helpfulness within in these pages, they come from the Lord.

If there is any relevance to current parent challenges that these pages have, it derives from the timeless principles of God's words of wisdom, especially in the Wisdom Literature of Scripture.

And if there is any sharpened awareness of how to apply these principles, it has been honed by scores of teachers and administrators in ACSI seminars, graduate students in the school counseling graduate program at Columbia International University, my friends at the Christian Counseling and Educational Foundation, and scores of teens who've said, "Get out of my face," in one way or another. All of these have been iron sharpening iron in my life (Proverbs 27:17).

Notably, honor goes to my wife for her co-partnership with our own kids and her patience while I've written, rewritten, and rewritten some more. Thanks too for the extraordinary craftsmanship of my editor Kevin Meath, the enthusiastic support of Rick Irvin of Shepherd Press, pastors, other school counselors, youth ministers (too numerous to mention), and especially that of my co-counselor at Delaware County Christian School, Renae Pieters.

The Lamb in the center of the throne deserves all the glory for any richness that is here. It is his cross that gives hope for accomplishing anything of promise with angry teens. They are not lost causes. The gospel's power unleashed can transform them. May the light of his Word through these pages transcend the weaknesses in the vessel who has written about it here and in those who seek to walk by it with the young people entrusted to them by the Wonderful Counselor.

PREFACE

Here's a fact.
Angry, unmotivated, and disinterested teens, whether Christian or not, are confused, insecure, and often blind to everything except what they want right now. Their desires and actions have been corrupted and polluted by sin. ***That's why they have a problem.***

Here's another fact.
Angry, unmotivated, and disinterested teens, whether Christian or not, are made in the image of God. This means that beneath their corrupted desires and actions the image of God remains. ***That's the key to solving their problem.***

Far from dismissing or sugar-coating sin, this approach opens wide the door to evangelizing the unsaved teen and to helping the Christian teen grow in holiness and wisdom. This book will teach you how to build a bridge to young adults on the basis of the ways in which their desires and actions reflect the image of God and the blessing of common grace.

1

THERE IS GOOD REASON
FOR HOPE

After thirty years as a high-school counselor, I know exactly what *Get outta my face!* looks like. After raising six teenagers, I have endured seasons where I had to live with that attitude, day in and day out. I've had plenty of angry, unmotivated, or disinterested teens send me the same clear message. Usually, they don't even need to speak. Whatever I may be trying to help them with, their expression says it all: *Get outta my face! I don't want to hear another word.*

Having talked with hundreds of parents, counselors, and youth workers over the years, I know I'm not alone in this. Nearly all of us stumble from time to time when we try to talk to an angry or upset teen. Am I suggesting it's our fault when one of them gives us a *Get outta my face* response? Not completely. But the vast majority of the time, it is preventable. Those walls that go up so easily between adults and teens certainly involve sin on the teen's part. Yet I'm convinced that most of us who try to reach young adults are completely unaware of the profound and extensive counsel Scripture offers us—counsel that can often keep those walls from going up in the first place.

The good news of this book is that it is not difficult to learn how to reach teens. In the following pages I attempt to unpack some of the rich, timeless wisdom of Proverbs and other sections of Scripture that God has given to equip us. As you continue reading, you will learn:

- How to talk effectively to an angry, disinterested, or unmotivated teen (who usually doesn't want to talk to you)
- How to nurture this young person's willingness to make better choices (when he or she often doesn't think that other options make any sense)
- How to restore a rich relationship (when both adult and teen may have given up hope that the relationship can get better)

The truths in this book are not new. They are rooted in the 2,000- and 3,000-year-old wisdom of the New Testament and the book of Proverbs. Remarkably, many youth counselors,* advisors to parents, and public-school counselors and educators now use *some* of these principles to help angry and at-risk teens. In most cases, however, they do not know where these truths come from or why they work so well. Therefore they have no idea how to use them to produce anything more than a temporary, external change—nor would they be able to in many non-Christian settings such as public schools.

But Christian parents can be encouraged to know that the Designer has shown us in Scripture how to talk effectively to anyone made in his own image—even teens whose sin breaks out in anger, bitterness, complacency, rebellion, defiance, or disinterest. The Bible's testimony about God's Word being a "light" and a "lamp" for his people (Psalm 119:120) is not vague idealism. *Get Outta*

---

*Some of the most prominent practitioners who have written, without particular interest in biblical principles, but whose writing shows the influence of the good sense that God makes possible in working with angry teens are Steve de Shazer, John Murphy, John Sharry, and Linda Metcalf.

My Face! aims to summarize common experiences parents have with angry teens and illustrate how biblical principles can bring remarkably clear and useful light to these situations. The aim is to position these truths on the bottom shelf so we can all reach them and put them to use with angry, unmotivated teens—even if we've made serious mistakes in our previous efforts. We all want to help these young people recognize their self-destructive ways, learn new and effective methods of dealing with life, and ultimately come into a deep and life-changing relationship with Christ. That's the goal of this book.

Who You Will Meet Throughout These Pages

In this book, you'll meet parents and teens who were at their wits' end with each other until they both began to make different decisions. The parents changed how they were approaching their teens, and the teens reevaluated whether their choices were really helping them get what they truly wanted. Here are a few of the people and some of the common themes you'll read about.

- Sarah's mom says her daughter is increasingly disrespectful and doing less and less school work. "Whenever I try to talk to her she gets angry and just shuts down. If I bring up anything having to do with the Lord, she just rolls her eyes."
- Bill's dad pleads for help. "When I try to talk to Bill about the things that we get into arguments about, he won't talk to me. I try to explain the reasons for my decisions but he just tunes me out. If there is any reaction, it's just to get into another argument. Then he ends up blaming me for not understanding and not listening. He usually goes to his room or to the rec room muttering something like, 'I can't talk to you!'"
- Sue is a sophomore in high school who has been thrown out of class for her disrespectful speech. "The teacher is so unreasonable about the way she grades . . . She has

these perfectionistic standards for everyone. No one agrees with the way she grades. I just couldn't take it anymore. She's so unreasonable."

- John is a junior who "just won't do anything," his mom said. "He is just so unmotivated. We've taken everything away from him. He's lost everything but still won't do any of his work."
- Emily is fifteen, and as big as her mom. She says that her mom "just yells and won't listen. She gets loud and yells at everything. She makes up all kinds of rules and doesn't give me any space. She blabs my business all over the neighborhood." Her mom says, "Emily is physically and verbally abusive with me and her sisters. She has made poor choices in friends and is just out of control—in my face with yelling and cursing."
- Mark and his dad got into an angry wrestling match on the kitchen floor. The dad, outweighing Mark by seventy-five pounds, soon had his son pinned. "Ok, I give up, just let me go!" Mark appealed. They got up and Mark stormed out of the kitchen muttering, "I hate this family. I can't wait to get outta here!" His dad went into the family room, thinking "Lord, what just happened?"

The Importance of Presentation

We are not responsible for the reactions of our teens. At the same time, *the way we approach them* will generally have a direct effect on how they choose to respond to us. Utilizing the principles summarized in this book can dramatically reduce negative reactions, and thus keep the walls from going up. This holds true for teens who *are* angry as a chronic condition and with teens who *get* angry on occasion. Our approach should be essentially the same whether we are dealing with a teen who is angry nearly all the time, or a normally open and sensitive teen who just happens to be angry at the moment. In this book, phrases such as "angry teen" refer to both categories of young person. The concepts offered here can help you communicate and encourage change in either situation.

A basic principle of this book is that *your first words to an angry teen will strongly push that interaction toward one of two outcomes:* your words being received, thus beginning a conversation, or a *Get outta my face* response, thus shutting it all down. Presentation, the way we approach our teen and start to talk, can make or break effective communication.

A good lesson on the importance of presentation appeared in *The Cosby Show*, whose lead character was Dr. Cliff Huxtable, played by Bill Cosby. In one episode, Cliff's daughter Vanessa had just come home after a semester at college. Out of nowhere, she announced that she was engaged to a young man whom her parents had never met. His name was Dabnes. He was a graduate of the college Vanessa attended, and now worked with its maintenance crew. Half an hour later, Vanessa unexpectedly brought Dabnes into the Huxtables' home to meet the family and have dinner with them.

Dabnes presented himself well. He seemed intelligent and was well-dressed, polite, friendly, and respectful. The problem was Vanessa's surprise announcement and the understandable shock it produced in her parents. Their contempt for the engagement was obvious.

Toward the end of dinner, Dr. Huxtable had the following conversation with Dabnes in an effort to explain why he felt as he did.

"You have a favorite food?"

"Yes sir, what you had here was fine. I especially enjoyed the fish sticks."

"No no, forget the fish sticks. I mean, do you have a favorite food, something that you really, you know, love?"

"Oh yeah. On occasion I enjoy a nice juicy steak."

"Steak! Steak, there you go. You've got the steak. Now just imagine we got the Porterhouse."

"OK."

"Porterhouse, and no white lines in it at all."

"Yeah."

"Now what would you like to go along with it?"

"Oh, uh, some crispy potatoes."

"No problem. Now, you got mushrooms. Mushrooms. Do you like your mushrooms?"

"Yes, sir."

"You can smell it, can't you?"

"Yeah!"

"Can you smell the potatoes?"

"Yes, sir."

"Smell the mushrooms?"

"Yes, sir."

"Sautéed."

"Smell good?"

"Mm, boy."

"Mm, hmm."

"Huh?"

"Yes, sir."

"All right. Now, I'm going to present it to you, right? I go over. I don't get a plate."

"Uh huh."

"I take the garbage can lid."

Dabnes falls silent.

"And I turn it upside down after taking it off of the garbage can. I take your steak, your potatoes, and your sautéed mushrooms, and I give it to you. Not too appetizing, is it? *It's in the presentation.* That's the way she brought you here. On a garbage can lid."[1]

After offering this little parable, Cliff began mending fences with Dabnes, but the point was made. Vanessa's unwise, surprising, and alarming announcement had created an unnecessary hurdle in the relationship between her parents and Dabnes. The same dynamic is at work in our parenting and youth ministry. The best and most valuable counsel we can possibly offer to our teen will be unappetizing if we don't give careful attention to how we present it.

Getting the Conversation Started

Get Outta My Face! shows parents, youth counselors, teachers, and other teen workers how to make contact with the kind of angry, needy young people whom adults most often come across: *those who are not looking for our help.* The following pages discuss some of the key guidance God has given us in his Word for speaking effectively to young adults. Utilizing these principles will often get their attention, hold their attention, eliminate their "push back," obtain their commitment to change, produce rapid positive change, and provide an entrée to the heart—our most critical target. Sound too good to be true? It would be if these principles were not in sync with how God has made us. It would be if God did not teach us in his Word how to employ these principles. But he has both formed these principles in us, and taught us how to use them for our good.

These principles are not an ironclad guarantee of success with every teen. Like us, teens are individuals made in God's image. They are not some unusually sophisticated machine that can be programmed or managed by behavior modification techniques or verbal gimmicks. There is essentially just one thing that will determine how a particular teen responds to your use of these principles. Ultimately, he will respond *on the basis of what he wants.* The principles shared in this book often work because they allow you to connect to angry and unmotivated teens via the wants and desires of their hearts. Much more will be said about this in chapter 3.

This book has a narrow focus and a limited goal. It does not present a full-scale method of youth counseling or parenting. Nor does it show parents how to hold their teens accountable for their foolish choices. Others have done these things quite well. This book brings principles of the biblical Wisdom Literature primarily to the front end of the conversations you need to have with angry or complacent teens. Its purpose is to equip parents and others to take the initiative as communicators with teens who probably don't want to talk.

Solomon himself affirms the importance of the approach you will find in this book.

- "The *tongue of the wise commends knowledge* [i.e., makes it attractive or appealing], but the mouths of fools pour out folly" (Proverbs 15:2, emphasis added).
- "The wise of heart is called discerning, and *sweetness of speech* increases persuasiveness" (Proverbs 16:21, emphasis added).
- "The heart of the wise makes his *speech judicious and adds persuasiveness* to his lips" (Proverbs 16:23, emphasis added).
- "A word *fitly spoken* is like apples of gold in a setting of silver" (Proverbs 25:11, emphasis added).

Most of us have been on the giving (and receiving) end of the unhelpful counsel illustrated in Proverbs 25:20: "Whoever sings songs to a heavy heart is like one who takes off a garment on a cold day, and like vinegar on soda." This out-of-touch kind of talk leaves the young person "cold" or makes him feel like he's being offered empty, unsubstantial froth.

Get Outta My Face! describes how to get the conversation started with these teens. Part III gives further guidance for making the changes permanent. Permanent change, of course, involves the heart and not just behavior. It's a "truth" matter that the Spirit alone can bring to lodge in our teen's heart so that he may be "set free" (John 8:32) from the angry, complacent, self-destructive, and hurtful patterns of his life.

Who This Book Is For

This book is for weak and sinful parents and youth workers, people just like you and me. If you are in any degree limited by your humanity, affected by your own sinful nature, or troubled by any of your past mistakes in trying to talk to your teen, this book is for you. The principles here are timeless, cross-cultural, cross-gender, and not limited by learning disabilities or ADHD diagnoses. Such factors may need to be taken into consideration, but they do not in the least render the Word of God ineffective.

Bringing our weakness and sinfulness to this process will make it easier to demonstrate genuine respect for the teen we are trying to help. The techniques presented in this book are not a means of manipulating teens. Without genuine respect, however, they can be perceived as manipulation and will likely backfire. The absence of a sincere, humble, and loving regard for the teen can earn charges like, "You are just a hypocrite," "You are trying to control me," "You don't understand me," or "You just want to use me to do what you want." The father's counsel in Proverbs 10:9 is applicable: "Whoever walks in integrity walks securely, but he who makes his ways crooked will be found out." Teens will quickly detect Mom's, Dad's, or any counselor's genuineness by their humility. Let us recall that we are weak people speaking to other weak people, who simply happen to be younger than us. Perfection is not the requirement for building a good communication bridge with our teen. Paul Tripp, in *Age of Opportunity: A Biblical Guide to Parenting Teens,* tells us how important this consciousness is for parents. "Remember, it is not your weaknesses that will get in the way of God's working through you, but your delusions of strength. His strength is made perfect in our weakness! Point to his strength by being willing to admit your weakness."[2]

More about this openness and how the Lord can use it will come up in chapter 4. It is sufficient to note here that these principles, like the rest of biblical revelation, are for weak, broken, inconsistent, imperfect people who are also redeemed and indwelt by God's Holy Spirit. Because of God's grace, despite all our inadequacies, we are able to employ the truths of Scripture to love and help angry and unmotivated young people.

What's in the Rest of This Book

The balance of Part I will present Scripture's true and accurate view of your angry or unmotivated teen, so that you might adopt the biblical view as your own. Part I will also ask you to assess your own heart motives and self-awareness. These opening chapters are foundational. They will set the stage for you to begin a conversation with your teen, even if he doesn't want to talk. The principles set forth in these initial chapters must be in place if you are to withstand the challenges that are likely to come as you apply the process explained in Part II.

Part II is the "how-to" section. Each of its four chapters explains one of the four features that make up the conceptual core of this book. I have used the letters LCLP throughout the book as a way to remember them.

> L is for Listen Big
> C is for Clarify Narrow
> L is for Look Wide
> P is for Plan Small

These four chapters explain and illustrate the LCLP principles using a variety of teen and parent vignettes. Several of these narratives are carried on from one chapter to the next so readers may get a more comprehensive sense of how the process works.

The first two parts of this book are concerned exclusively with surface motivations and external behavior. When dealing with angry or unmotivated teens, this is where the process must begin. As Christians, however, we know that this is not where the process ought to end. Changes that are rooted purely in external behavior will not last. Therefore, Part III explains how to use the bridge of communication you will have constructed in Part II to help address your teen's heart issues.

The LCLP principles you will learn in this book can build a surprisingly strong and reliable bridge of communication to your teen. But communication itself is not the ultimate goal. It is merely a means to a much higher and greater goal: to lead your teen to the cross, whether for the first time or in pursuit of a deeper and more meaningful understanding of the work of Christ.

The goal of any biblical counseling is the glory of God. Christian parents, teachers, counselors, and other youth workers want to see God's name be hallowed, his kingdom come, and his will be done. They want to see the power of the gospel unleashed in teens' lives, that Jesus Christ might become their Pearl of Great Price. That is the aim of this book. May the Wonderful Counselor be pleased to use this tool for his glory as he frees spiritual captives and makes them his own.

> And the Lord's servant must not be quarrelsome but kind to everyone, able to teach, patiently enduring evil, correcting his opponents with gentleness. God may perhaps grant them repentance leading to a knowledge of the truth, and they may escape from the snare of the devil, after being captured by him to do his will.
>
> —2 Timothy 2:24–26

2

UNDERSTANDING YOUR TEEN BIBLICALLY

The message on Greg's office voicemail was from his wife. The topic was a familiar one.

"Greg, would you talk to Sarah again about her attitude and behavior? Please do it this evening if you can. She's become more and more disrespectful and is doing less and less school work. Whenever I try to talk to her she gets angry and shuts down. If I bring up anything having to do with the Lord, she just rolls her eyes. Please don't tell her that I called or she'll be really mad."

Is there a way Greg can talk to Sarah and elicit something better than a *Get outta my face* response? How could a youth worker* go about helping Sarah?

Can either of them expect Sarah to ask for help on her own? Not likely. Will she be open to talk about the disrespect she has shown toward her mom? Probably not. Is she a Christian? Based

---

*Throughout this book, "youth worker" will serve as shorthand for any non-family member whose role includes efforts to help teens. This may be a school counselor, youth group leader, youth pastor, or other youth counselor. The assumption is that these youth workers are able to freely discuss the Bible and faith. When I refer either to a Christian school or a youth group setting, please understand that these are interchangeable.

on her attitude, it's hard to tell. Even if she makes a profession of faith, is she motivated to do Christ's will right now and at home and at school? It doesn't look that way.

Is she likely to welcome any discussion about her attitudes and behavior? Or about the things she's doing to hurt herself and others? Or about the example she is setting for her sisters, others at school, or in the youth group? Probably not. Will an immediate attempt to use the Bible to address her attitudes or words of disrespect bring her to a broken and repentant spirit? In all probability, she'll see any such offers "to help" as "just one more lecture" by someone "trying to change me" who "just doesn't understand me."

Angry and unmotivated teens can and do think. But they do not do it with the maturity, responsibility, and spiritual commitment that Christian parents and caring youth workers consider to be vital. Sarah's universe is more circumscribed, and she is at its center. The Bible recognizes this to be true of such seething or simmering young people. But it does not offer us feeble or benign counsel as we face them. It coaches us in skillful ways to talk to them, serve them, and motivate them.

Eight Biblical Lenses for Seeing Our Angry Teens Clearly

Godly wisdom for helping these teens comes through a series of teachings or principles that work like lenses. When we peer through these lenses at our teens we find a way to talk to them, connect with them, and motivate them to make biblically wise choices. When parents or youth workers use the biblically crafted approach explained in this book, angry young people will usually see them as respectful, helpful, and worth listening to. Remarkably, the teens will usually come back for more of the same.

Too good to be true? Not at all. "When a man's ways please the LORD, he makes even his enemies to be at peace with him" (Proverbs 16:7). This is not an absolute promise, of course. Jesus' own life *and death* bears that out. But the principle almost always holds true. If we view our angry teens as God describes them, and if we relate to them as he counsels us, we can be agents of our teens' peace—in their relationships with other people and in their relationship with God.

1. *Teens, just like parents and counselors, are sinners.*

What a negative way to start!

It may seem so at first. But there is rich hope in an accurate diagnosis. Some time ago a man had a serious gallbladder problem. He was scheduled for surgery, sedated, and operated on. He woke up in the recovery room to discover no abdominal scar, but a shorter leg and large bandage where his left foot had been. A gross misdiagnosis of this man's problem by the attending surgeons and nurses led to a tragic loss for this man and a huge malpractice suit for the doctors and hospital. Misdiagnoses don't just leave real problems unfixed. They usually add new problems that further complicate an already difficult situation.

The Bible affirms that we are sinners. In Romans 3:9–18, the apostle Paul concludes the first section of his letter by piling Old Testament quotation upon quotation to prove this point about us all.

> For we have already charged that all . . . are under sin, as it is written: "None is righteous, no, not one; no one understands; no one seeks for God. All have turned aside; together they have become worthless; no one does good, not even one." "Their throat is an open grave; they use their tongues to deceive." "The venom of asps is under their lips." "Their mouth is full of curses and bitterness." "Their feet are swift to shed blood; in their paths are ruin and misery, and the way of peace they have not known." "There is no fear of God before their eyes."

What a description! A few verses further on he says, "For all have sinned and fall short of the glory of God" (3:23). No teen or adult escapes this declaration. Each of us has broken God's very first command: "You shall have no other gods before me" (Exodus 20:3). We have erected all kinds of imitation gods for ourselves. We often live contentedly without the Lord or any reference to his purpose. He wants us to live for him and his glory, to be at his disposal, and to be satisfied with him. Paul urges us all to cast this big net of concern for his glory over all of our choices when he says, "whether you eat or drink, or whatever you do, do all to the glory of God" (1 Corinthians 10:31).

Angry teens (as well as angry parents and youth workers) must recognize that their will is not at the center of any universe except in their own imagination. But that vaunted, seemingly essential, and completely imaginary epicenter is precisely where they have placed themselves. Someone is not respecting *them*, giving *them* what *they* want, appreciating *them*, helping *them*, understanding *them*, or accepting *them*. James acknowledges that this is the source of anger:

> What causes quarrels and what causes fights among you? Is it not this, that your passions are at war within you? *You desire and do not have, so you murder. You covet and cannot obtain, so you fight and quarrel.* You do not have, because you do not ask.
>
> —James 4:1–2, emphasis added

If we understand that our teen's self-absorbed choices, as well our own, give birth to our "quarrels" and "fights," three very good things can happen. We can stop being defensive. We can stop being idealistic. We can stop being hopeless.

First, we can stop being defensive. We won't need to jealously protect our own sense of perfection or our teenager's. Such innocence is a naïve, humanistic illusion; everyone else knows we're sinners. Looking through the scriptural lens of universal sinfulness allows us to see accurately enough to admit it. We can, do, and will make serious, horrible choices. Don't be surprised by them. We're sinners. So are our teens.

Second, we can stop being idealistic. We will recognize that our kids can do any sinful thing that we older sinners can do. Neither parenting, Christian education, heritage, nor fine church involvement can alter anyone's essential sin nature. To lie, make self-centered choices, be destructive, or be deeply hurtful to oneself or others may be "out of character," but it is not outside of any human being's nature. Paul's summary statement in Romans 3:23 makes it clear that every feature of our personality, intellect, emotions, and wills has been infected by sin. Seeing ourselves and our teens as sinners allows us to see everyone more accurately, and helps us resist the temptation to speak with self-righteous condemnation.

Finally, we can stop being hopeless. Seeing our teens as sinners also positions us to aim for the hope of gospel healing in the deepest parts of their being as we interact with them. As this book will emphasize and demonstrate, there is a time to discuss heart issues, repentance, and the richness of Christ's sufficient, gracious acceptance and forgiveness. But that will normally have to follow our initial, respectful conversations that address surface levels. Recognizing our teen's sinful identity, however, does keep us alert to the fact that helping him with anger or motivation is not an end. It is an avenue to his heart for the enduring change that the gospel alone can create.

2. *Teens can be respected as young adults.*

The Hebrew word na'ar, translated "youth" or "young," occurs more than 250 times in the Old Testament. It is usually applied to young people between puberty and their early thirties. Joseph, a seventeen-year-old in Genesis 37:2, and young Daniel and his friends in Daniel 1:4–6 are called na'ar. Solomon also used the term for the "youth" to whom he addressed the book of Proverbs (1:4). The counsel he gives in Proverbs is for older as well as younger adults. They both have the same capacities for decision-making and both are accountable for their choices, but the young adults don't have the same freedom that full adults have. That will come with age. They are still under the authority of their parents.

From the wide range of topics Solomon brings to the attention of young adults, it is clear that the teens and "twenty-somethings" he addresses are people who are real and make real choices. Pick any section of Proverbs and scan the topics that Solomon is including for teens to think and decide about. Subjects include truthfulness and lying, good and harmful friendships, sexual immorality and purity, greediness and generosity, hard work and laziness, integrity and duplicity, good and bad reputations, honor and dishonor to parents and other authorities, helpful and hurtful speech, and variations of these and other topics.

When a parent interacts with an angry young person—let's call her Sarah—the parent may include large doses of affirmation about the identity Sarah has as a young adult. Sarah can think and she can make choices—real choices. She's not a child anymore, regardless of how "childish" her choices may seem. Such recognition of Sarah's young adulthood is not likely to change her right now. However, it does give parents and youth workers the opportunity to speak positively, encouragingly, and accurately to her. This may catch her off guard because of the blame she's accustomed to hearing, the guilt she's used to feeling, and the disrespect she so often senses. Affirming her adulthood will affect parent and child, youth worker and teen, and will begin a new process of communication.

3. *Common grace, God's general goodness to all, allows any sinner to make some wise choices.*

However horrible Sarah's behavior is (or, for that matter, any other sinner's), she is still capable of making wise choices. God has created her in his image, and by virtue of being his human creature she can make good decisions.

It is true that every aspect of Sarah's character has been infected by sin. Paul made that clear in his letter to the Romans cited above. But it is equally true that God has endowed Sarah and everyone else, believer or unbeliever, and even people within pagan cultures, to make some choices that allow them to live orderly and enjoyable lives. Egyptian sun worshipers could teach Moses culture, literature, mathematics, and management. In God's time, this knowledge would help Moses to lead Israel. Babylonian officials could teach Daniel and his young teenage friends about the language, culture, law, and government of their pagan captors. Their training would position them to function as significant civil authorities in that country and put the true God of the Covenant on display before the world of that day. Greek and Roman emperors and governors could create roads, spread peace and education, make international travel possible, and create laws that would later be used to speed the spread of the gospel.

Sarah, too, can make good decisions. She can make poor ones, of course, but the lens of Scripture confronts us with the fact that there is more to a teen than her sinful choices. These sinful choices should not be minimized. But wise interaction with an angry teen will mean that we keep in mind and share our belief with her that she does have the capacity to make wise decisions—if she wants to.

4. God's goodness accounts for "wise wants" that lie (often deeply) within our teens.

People want peace, love, joy, and acceptance by God (or a god). These are some of the "wise wants" that God has wired into our natures. Teens appreciate beauty, fairness, justice, sacrifice, and kindness. They value truthfulness, integrity, loyalty, freedom, and respect. The list of virtues they esteem, to one extent or another, goes on and on. This does not mean they practice these things. Their self-centeredness, like ours, gets in the way of being what they want underneath.

In its naked and unrestrained form, our sin would destroy us and everyone else. But such uninhibited, total abandonment to one's own self-glorification never reaches full flower in any of us. Something restrains us. By common grace, there is in everyone some measure of respect for virtue. Paul refers to this general human desire by noting that "the requirements of the law are written on their [and our] hearts" (Romans 2:14–15). The sense of the moral law of God—that which is right, admirable, and desirable—is imprinted on each of us as creatures of God.

These desires are in angry teens too. In Proverbs 10:4, for example, Solomon says, "A slack hand causes poverty, but the hand of the diligent makes rich." When parents are urged to reason with their youth about laziness and poverty, they can do so because the connection between diligence and wealth makes sense to young people. All of the proverbs have assumptions of "wise wants" like this lying beneath them.

One more example may make these assumptions more visible. Solomon's counsel that "sweetness of speech increases persuasiveness" (Proverbs 16:21) may make sense to a teen with a caustic, sarcastic tongue because she probably wants to be persuasive. She wants people to see things her way. She'll be able to compare the effects of the speech and language she uses with the effects that "sweetness" produces.

More will be said in the next chapter regarding this important scriptural assumption about young people. Learning how to tune into these wise wants will set the stage for you to communicate with your teen because you are appealing to what is motivating her—some constructive, God-imprinted desires, whether she recognizes God as their author or not.

5. Help that brings about change in angry teens often begins at a surface level but must aim deeper.

Sarah may want to be out with her friends, whom her mom doesn't trust. Or she may want to buy a pair of pants that her mom doesn't consider modest. Let's assume that some wise wants lie beneath Sarah's choices. What might those be? For example, Sarah may want to have rich relationships with others, a good reputation among her peers (however she happens to define "good" in this case), or to be treated as a mature, responsible, trustworthy, respectable young adult by her mother. Let's also assume that Sarah's mother is able to speak with her daughter in terms of wise wants. If Sarah's mom reasons with her about the friends or the pants in this way, Sarah may be willing to make some other, better decisions. Thus, an angry interchange may be avoided.

But even though this scenario is preferable to another argument, Sarah's heart motives have yet to be addressed. Just like the rest of us, her passions and the desires that drive her are linked to the god or gods to which she has wed herself. There is good reason why John concludes his first letter with the command to "keep yourselves from idols" (1 John 5:21). We all have a problem with them.

Ultimately, for Sarah not to be an angry person, she will need to realign her life with the God who is, and submit to his will for her decisions. But that discussion can't happen effectively right now. Sarah is not ready to talk about her gods, and any such talk is likely to invite a resentful response.

But her mom *can* begin talking about the surface things in Sarah's life—the things she wants such as the pleasure of relationships, and respect and reputation as a mature person. Jesus did this often. He began with essentially surface-level "felt needs" and then directed the conversation toward more serious heart matters.

How many thousands did Jesus heal, feed, and teach who did not end up following him? He went about doing good, notwithstanding peoples' responses. In these and other examples, Jesus demonstrated God's goodness to all humankind. As his followers, we are called to pattern our motives and actions after his. We are called to show love to everyone, even our own angry teens. Our love is not to be conditioned upon the way they respond to us, appreciate us, respect us, or accept us. "Love your enemies . . . that you may be sons of your Father in heaven. He causes his sun to rise on the evil and the good, and sends rain on the righteous and the unrighteous" (Matthew 4:44–45). Here, Jesus himself tells us to imitate the Father in the way we meet the surface needs of others.

The book of Proverbs—God's manual for counseling teens—urges this same generous viewpoint. It suggests that we reach out to foolish, immature, angry, rebellious, lazy, and unconcerned youth at the surface level of their motives with outward, behavior-changing counsel. These are conversations about wise wants.

The ultimate goal is clearly a heart-level "fear of the Lord" which is "the beginning of wisdom" (9:10). This is where our conversations must eventually lead. But the heavy emphasis in Proverbs on external behavior for the purpose of producing certain practical results clearly legitimizes an approach to counseling that begins with surface concerns. For angry or unmotivated kids, generally this is the only place our efforts can begin fruitfully.

Our love does not sweep under the carpet any of our teen's foolish choices. We must hold them accountable. This book is about how to do that in a respectful way that often opens up communication with them, communication that makes real heart change possible.

6. Teens can and must think about their choices in light of goals and consequences.

Scripture often emphasizes the seriousness of something by repeating it. God only needs to say something once for it to be true, of course, but when God repeats himself once, twice, or several times, we know that this is something he *really* does not want us to miss.

So what does it mean if God says something, in one way or another, more than 250 times? This is exactly what he does when he teaches us through his Word how to make decisions.

Translators of the NIV make it clear that young adults are thinking people. They use many variations of the words "wise," "prudent," "understand," "discretion," "discern," "know," "discipline" (which is related to training and learning), and "instruction." More than 250 times the writers of Proverbs refer to intellectual activity as indispensable to sound, godly decision-making. In addition, nearly 700 times Proverbs urges teens to think about their choices in light of the positive and negative outcomes of their decisions.

Angry teens *can* think. Proverbs tells us how we can encourage them to do so in a way that will be profitable.

Perhaps you have thought of Proverbs 3:5–6, which tells young people to "lean not on your own understanding." That, of course, is true. It is quite different, however, from suggesting that young people ought not to *use* their understanding. Indeed, Proverbs 1:8 says "Listen, my son, to your father's instruction and do not forsake your mother's teaching," and Proverbs 3:1 says, "My son, do not forget my teaching." Proverbs 1:28 warns against hating knowledge. In other words, teens should be thoughtful and intellectually proactive. The alternative is the intellectual laziness of complacency, and "complacency . . . destroy[s]" (1:32).

None of us should lean on our own understanding. But the Bible is a book of knowledge. It teaches us that certain choices bring about certain consequences. In order to take advantage of this knowledge we obviously must *employ* our understanding.

7. *Scriptural principles cover both* how *to speak and* what *to say to angry, unmotivated teens.*

The Bible's principles cover all of life. Paul asserts this in 2 Timothy 3:16–17 when he says, "All Scripture is breathed out by God and profitable for teaching, for reproof, for correction, and for training in righteousness, that the man of God may be competent, equipped for every good work." Paul tells young Pastor Timothy that Scripture gives him all the resources he'll need for working with people who are "lovers of self, lovers of money, proud, arrogant, abusive, disobedient to their parents, ungrateful, unholy, heartless, unappeasable, slanderous, without self-control, brutal, not loving good, treacherous, reckless, swollen with conceit, lovers of pleasure rather than lovers of God" (2 Timothy 3:2–5). This is both a dramatic and a surprisingly accurate description of many angry teens.

In our knowledge of God, he gives us resources for "all things that pertain to life and godliness" (2 Peter 1:3). The phrase "life and godliness" encompasses matters involving our relationships with others and our relationship with God. As a "lamp to my feet and a light to my path" (Psalm 119:105), God's Word is truly a resource of illumination. His Word is a resource of life, for we cannot rely upon "bread alone" (Matthew 4:4) for our sustenance. Everything in this creation rusts, rips, breaks, fades, fails, gets moldy, and ultimately disappoints and passes away. But God's Word is a resource of permanence; it is the exception which "will not pass away" (Matthew 24:35). The Word of God is also a resource of sanctification and character change. Jesus identified the instrument that the Father would use to produce such change when he prayed, "Sanctify [change] them by your truth. Your word is truth" (John 17:17). Truly, every other basis for advice or counsel about living is like urging a loved one to "build his house upon the sand" (Matthew 7:26–27).

The Bible does not teach us to search its pages to see what every nuance of human behavior should look like. It does instruct us, however, to think about how to apply the principles of Scripture in every area of life. When it comes to helping angry teens, the hard work of thinking, careful review of the Scriptures, and thoughtful study belong to the biblical counselor and the thoughtful parent. The fact that we have to think about how to apply the Word of God to specific circumstances does not diminish the richness of God's revelation in the least. On the contrary, we have reason to marvel at its richness, robustness, sturdiness, and profoundness. God created us as real people with the ability to think about our choices and to make decisions about everything, even our mundane eating and drinking, so that it results in his glory—"whether you eat or drink or whatever you do, do all to the glory of God" (1 Corinthians 10:31). The principles of his Word set the trajectory of our thinking in God-pleasing directions, including how to speak to our teens and the sorts of things we need to say. These how-to-speak and what-to-say issues are at the heart of *Get Outta My Face!*

8. God gives us others to support us and to help us counsel our teens.

"Where there is no guidance, a people falls, but in an abundance of counselors there is safety" (Proverbs 11:14). The word for "guidance" in this verse is a nautical term. It refers to skill in handling the ropes of a ship. This is also the term used in Proverbs 1:5 describing one purpose of the book of Proverbs: "let the wise hear and increase in learning, and the one who understands obtains guidance." Proverbs is God's manual for training us to handle the ropes of parenting young adults—and, of course, of managing ourselves wisely.

Helping angry teens requires several "rope skills": listening, understanding, communicating respect, and leading toward solutions. Part II of this book will focus on developing these skills. But just as in sailing, more hands than our own may be required to steer the craft safely and effectively. That's why God intends us to be part of the larger family of his church. In the passage above, Solomon shows the wisdom of having such a set of relationships when he states that "in an abundance of counselors there is safety."

In every area of the Christian life, growth is a community affair, not a private one. In Romans, Paul states that we are "members one of another" (12:5). In 1 Corinthians, he affirms there are ". . . many parts, yet one body" (12:20). And in Ephesians he explains that "when each part is working properly, [they] make the body grow so that it builds itself up in love" (4:16). God has given us a community of brothers and sisters whom he intends us to lean upon for help as we come up against some of the difficulties of parenting teens.

As a teenager, one of our six children pushed Betty and me past the limits of our parental understanding. He was angry, violent, destructive, and disrespectful. All we had learned in raising our four older children seemed to count for nothing. The police, the courts, jail, and even crisis-center people made no impact upon him. Our church, however, played an indispensable role. They encouraged us, supported us in our actions, prayed for us, and stuck with us. They were God's instrument to alleviate our insecurities and fears, support us when faced with uncertainties about options, and weep and pray for us when we had to make heart-wrenching decisions. At the time when our son clearly became more than we could handle on our own, our family was part of a mainly African-American church. Betty and I are white, and the son with whom we were struggling is African-American. Throughout the entire trauma, our son was never able to use the "race card" as an excuse, rationalization, or accusation. The brothers and sisters in our church leadership team made sure of that. Our local body of Christ was in this with us, and was "in his face" at the proper times and in the proper ways to hold him accountable.

Your angry teen may push you past the limits of your understanding as well. God's church is an absolutely vital instrument for your support and growth through these difficult times. Counselors may help. Books like this one may help. Teachers may help. Residential programs may be able to help. But Christ's church is his designated, primary resource for your support in such challenges—regardless of how your son or daughter responds to your helping efforts.

Stop, Look, Listen: Learn

On January 12, 2007, at 7:51 a.m., world-renowned violin virtuoso Joshua Bell, dressed as a common street musician, played for forty-three minutes at the top of an indoor escalator system serving the L'Enfant Plaza subway station in Washington, DC. An artist who commands more than $1,000 a minute for his performances, Bell played six classical masterpieces on his $3.5 million Stradivari-designed violin from the early 18th century. More than 1,000 commuters hurried past Bell. Only a few gave him more than a passing glance, one recognized him from a concert she had been to the night before at the Library of Congress, and a grand total of $32.17 was tossed into his open violin case. In the presence of greatness, virtually no one recognized him and none honored him as arguably the greatest violinist in the world!

Joshua Bell was part of an experiment sponsored by the *Washington Post* to study how context affects the way people respond to a person or event. In other words, how does *what I'm looking for* affect what I see? Three days before, Bell had sold out Boston's stately Symphony Hall at $100 per ticket for a "pretty good" seat, according to the *Post* article. Those concert-goers had been expecting a spectacular artist and were duly rewarded. Indeed, every other time Joshua Bell plays his violin in public, people are astounded. But the busy, chilly commuters on that January morning, coming upon a violinist in jeans and a baseball cap playing for spare change, allowed their observations to take the path of least resistance. As a result, they saw what they expected to see: nothing particularly noteworthy.

What will you expect to see the next time you talk with your angry teen? If you look through the lenses God holds before us in his Word, you will see what you may not have noticed before, or perhaps have not noticed in a very long time. Rather than the conversational equivalent of hurrying past on your way to something more important you will stop, and look, and listen. This is someone whom God expects you to approach with love and respect and wisdom and thoughtful, careful, honest, biblical speech. When your teen senses that attention and regard from you, you can expect the uncommon reward of attentiveness. That is how the door begins to open, how the walls begin to come down, and how you can start to get past the *Get outta my face* response.

3

WISE WANTS

A POINT OF CONTACT

"When I try to talk with Bill, my teenage son, about the things that we get into arguments about, he seems to shut down. He won't talk to me. I try to explain the reasons for my decisions but he just tunes me out and won't talk about what he thinks. If there is any reaction, it's just to get into another argument. Then he ends up blaming me for not understanding and not listening. He usually goes to his room or to the rec room muttering something like, 'I can't talk to you!'"

Teens often won't talk to adults on their own about the things that "make them mad." They'll talk to each other readily enough, but not usually to the people who love them the most. This is not because they believe the parent doesn't love them, isn't cool, doesn't dress "acceptably," or doesn't speak teen lingo. It is because of whose "wants" the teen thinks mom or dad, the teacher or youth pastor is going to talk about. "Are you going to talk to me about what *you* want or what *I* want?"

Whose "want" we talk about with our teen is important. In the season of his anger—whether for a day, a week, a month, or longer—his words, speech, and decisions are being fueled by what he wants. James explains this function of our "wants." (We looked at this earlier, but it is worth revisiting.) "What causes quarrels and what causes fights among you? Is it not this, that your passions are at war within you? You desire and do not have, so you murder. You covet and cannot obtain, so you fight and quarrel" (4:1–2).

We all make choices based on what we want. There are no accidental choices. But when these choices become things we are passionate about, things we think we must have or absolutely need, we "quarrel," "fight," and "murder"—with our words and attitudes especially. This doesn't mean we are always fully aware of the motives behind our choices. But it does affirm that even our angriest choices could not be made and would not be made unless we intended to make them. Our decisions are not accidental, and they are not caused by other people, disappointing circumstances, or biochemical imbalances. We choose things because we want certain outcomes.

"What Do You Want?"

Jesus incorporated the "what do you want?" question into his work with people. Three of the gospel writers recount the story of blind men who were brought to Jesus outside of Jericho. While some of the details differ from account to account, in each of them Jesus first began his interaction with a question, "What do you want me to do?" (Matthew 20:32; Mark 10:51; Luke 18:41). Isn't what they would want obvious? They were blind! What would blind men want more than their sight? But this is where Jesus began.

Some time ago, Kim, a tenth grade girl, came storming into my office frustrated and upset at the grades she was getting in biology and two other subjects. She was new to the school and said she just wanted to leave. "I can't stand this school." I listened to her for a while, saw her frustration, and echoed it back to her. She didn't want to fail. She didn't want her dad to be mad at her for her grades. She wasn't making friends quickly, was lonely, and there was just too much homework. I asked, "Kim, what do you want?"

"I want a Jeep when I'm seventeen!"

I would have never guessed it. But it turned out that a Jeep was what her dad had promised her if she was on the honor roll each quarter in our school until she turned seventeen. Without knowing this I could have begun talking to her about the importance of her grades, what her grades on her transcript would say to a college admissions counselor, her responsibility to use her academic talents for the Lord, keeping her grades up so she wouldn't get the restrictions of academic probation, how having good grades would show respect for her parents, and lots of other eloquent and spiritually accurate reasons for doing her work. None of it would have mattered to Kim. She wanted a Jeep.

When Jesus asked the blind men, "What do you want?" he knew, of course, what they would say. He was asking this for their sakes and for ours. Whatever else this question did, it crystallized in the minds of those men exactly what it was they desired. In his ministry to them, Jesus began with what they wanted and went on to serve them from that point. Jesus did the same thing with James and John and their mother. The two men asked him to do "whatever they wanted" for them. Jesus asked, "What do you want me to do for you?" (Mark 10:36). They wanted to sit on his right and left hand in his kingdom. He said that wasn't possible to grant to them. He began with what they wanted, though, and used that as the jumping-off point for his counsel about servant-hood to them and, later, to the other disciples.

Wise Wants Are Underneath Most Teen Felt Wants

As I pointed out above, there are no accidental choices. However, given the common self-centeredness of the teen years and the way modern culture urges youth to do what they "feel," many of their decisions are simply rooted in their desires for the moment—their felt wants. At the same time, there is an *underlying* set of wants within every young person that is part of their human nature as a creature made in the image of God. These are their "wise wants." These wise wants and the "What do you want?" question which Jesus asked are implied in hundreds of points of counsel to young adults in Proverbs. We covered this briefly in chapter 2. But because this book will be of no use to you unless you understand the biblical principle of wise wants, I think it is important to discuss the concept a bit further.

Solomon teaches about our underlying motives in Proverbs 16:2. He asserts that "a man's ways seem right to him but motives are judged by the Lord." He is saying that:

1) we all *act* ("a man's ways");

2) we all have *thoughts about* our actions ("seem right to him"), and;

3) we all have *underlying motives* for our actions and thoughts ("but motives are judged . . .")

In the following verses, think about the underlying motives that Solomon presumes already exist:

"Lazy hands make a man poor, but diligent hands bring wealth" (10:4). The assumption is that teens want to avoid poverty and acquire wealth. A verse like this may help them to think twice about their laziness.

"A man is praised according to his wisdom, but men with warped minds are despised" (12:8). The assumption is that young people want praise, approval, and respect. In light of such a passage, teens may evaluate how their ideas will be seen by others.

These assumed desires are wise wants. Many of the proverbs assume that youth:

- want a reputation for trustworthiness and honor
- want their parents to be proud and joyful because of their choices
- want to have healthy friendships, including delightful romance
- want to live with a sense of security and confidence
- want to be useful in the lives of others
- want to be competent and successful in work

- want to earn a good living and be prosperous
- want to have a positive influence in the lives of others
- want to be discerning and thoughtful
- want to use good judgment
- want to be able to respond effectively to others' questions and demands
- want to combat laziness, selfishness, anger, lying, and lust
- want to not be seduced, exploited, deceived, or misled

In each of us, however, these embedded wise wants are contaminated by our sin nature. The wise King Solomon who makes these wise-want assumptions regarding young adults is not naïve. He knows the human heart has mixed motives. He writes, "Who can say, 'I have made my heart pure; I am clean from my sin?'" (Proverbs 20:9). Solomon's rhetorical question shows that he is not living in an idealistic or sentimental dream world about youth or anyone else. Without denying that youth are affected by sin, he still urges parents and others who work with youth to appeal to them with this: God offers hundreds of desirable outcomes for wise living.

Indeed, in Proverbs alone God offers nearly 700 examples of positive and negative physical, mental, emotional, and psychological consequences for wise or foolish decisions. Clearly there are spiritual benefits too, but by and large the outcomes for wise living in Proverbs are posed in terms of the here and now. This is why the pithy proverbs make sense to teens—because they resonate with the wise wants of their human nature. God has wired them, as creatures made in his image, to make these specific connections. Common grace is at work in the very core of who we are, teens included, causing us to want the advantages of wise living and not the disadvantages of foolish living.

The "Unmotivated" Teen Also Has Wise Wants

It's easy to see that angry teens are motivated by wants. But teens whom we label as "unmotivated" have wise wants driving them, too.

Mrs. Andrews and John were in my office because he had just been placed on academic probation. He'd been failing several courses for two quarters in a row. His mom's exasperation was written on her face and in the tone of her voice.

"John is just not motivated. He won't do anything that is good for him. He's grounded, can't use the car, now he's on academic probation and so is ineligible for wrestling, and we've restricted him on weekends so now he can't go out with his girlfriend. But nothing we do seems to make a difference. Nothing motivates him. We've even severely limited how much he can be at his job, which he loves. Nothing seems to work."

I looked at John and asked if his parents had indeed imposed all these restrictions on him. He said they had. Then I turned to his mother again and asked if I could share with her another perspective about what John was doing. She said that would be fine.

I turned to her son. "John, I don't mean to show disrespect to your mother, but I couldn't disagree with her more. I'm not sure I've ever seen a student more motivated than you are!"

He leaned forward a bit. I had his interest. Mom was genuinely perplexed.

"You're grounded and can't go out with friends, right?"

"Yes."

"You lost some time at your job because of your grades, right? You can't use the car, you're on academic probation, making you ineligible for wrestling, and you can't go out with your girlfriend?"

"Yeah, that's what they've said."

I looked at him and at his mom, paused, and then asked, "So with all these restrictions on you, you are still doing the things that made you lose these privileges. Is that what I'm hearing your mom say, John?"

He thought about his response and then slowly agreed that he was reacting in the way I had described.

"That is remarkable motivation," I said. "You want something so badly that you have committed yourself to enduring significant pain and loss in order to get it. You're willing to put up with all this discomfort to gain what you want. That is serious dedication, in my judgment, not lack of motivation. I can only imagine what you could do in your life, John, if you decided to use that kind of intensity and commitment to pursue things that could benefit you instead of things that are bringing you loss and trouble."

John was certainly motivated—but not to do what his mom wanted, what the youth pastor wanted, what the teachers wanted, what I wanted, or even what God wanted. He was motivated only to pursue his own wants. The warnings adults gave him and the pain that came from his choices didn't matter. He wanted something so badly he was willing to ignore warnings, pain, and loss of privileges. One youth counselor has said that he doesn't know if he's ever met an unmotivated teen.

A young person who will not pursue what the adults in his life want him to pursue is not necessarily unmotivated. He or she is probably highly motivated. The only question is: What is driving those motivations?

Jesus and Solomon Can Help You Avoid a Common Error

Godly moms and dads often think that to be faithful to the Lord in their parenting role, they are duty-bound to immediately confront their teen with his or her rebellion, self-centeredness, or disrespect. In the interview with John, for example, it is true that all of these sinful reactions may have been powerfully at work in his heart, fueling his academic stubbornness. But there is more to John than just these sinful responses. There are elements of wise wants in him as well. John wanted to be independent and make his own decisions, and he was committed to his goals. Yes, the way he was going about it was sinful, and his motives were undoubtedly mixed, but there were nevertheless some wise wants underlying his actions.

For parents, the best question to ask is not, "*Do* we deal with the sin or do we *not?*" The question is, "*When* and *how* is the sin to be dealt with in the way that will be most effective?" In Proverbs, the "fear of the Lord" is certainly the beginning of knowledge and wisdom (1:7; 9:10). But while "the fear of the Lord" is the heart orientation that *ought* to control all choices, the wise counselors in that book know that we are all flawed creatures in a fallen world. They do not demand a teen's commitment to the fear of the Lord before they give helpful counsel—counsel that often speaks far more directly to wise wants than it does to matters of spiritual conviction.

Solomon and his fellow sages are not the only ones willing to impart wisdom and instruction in this way. The teachings of Jesus demonstrate the value of communicating in stages. There was a "now" stage of his teaching when he walked among his disciples. But there was also a second stage. "I still have many things to say to you, but you cannot bear them now" (John 16:12). Do you see the implication here? His timetable was determined by *what they could bear.* They simply were not ready for everything all at once. Otherwise he would have told them while he was still on earth. Most people who have been Christians more than a few years can attest to a similar pattern in their own lives. God does not confront us with every area of sin and weakness in our lives in a single week. He works in stages, as we can bear it.

The goal of this book is to equip you to help your teens grasp the things about themselves that God wants them to notice just as Jesus and Solomon intended their hearers to grow in their understanding of wisdom for their lives. This will usually follow a slowly unfolding conversation that eventually allows you to talk more openly about matters of sin and sanctification. The pattern that Jesus gave us, as well as the counsel of Solomon, affirm the wisdom of beginning to talk with a teen in the domain *in which he is thinking*—not where we would like him to be. The blind men whom Jesus healed remind us that it is legitimate to start our counsel with what needy people *want*.

Our deep desire is to see our teens change because of love for Christ. However, the counsel that leads a disinterested or angry teen toward godly motives and choices usually cannot begin at a deep, heart level. In time, the connections we have with our teens may let us talk about these things. But often our conversation cannot start there. If you begin your conversation by reviewing their wise wants, that will probably do more than just get their attention. It will likely give both of you the ability to talk respectfully to one another and actually be heard.

4

YOUR STANCE

DETERMINE TO GLORIFY GOD

Mark and his father were wrestling on the kitchen floor, and it wasn't for fun.

The night before, Mark had come in well past his curfew. Lately he had been mouthy around the house, and had been letting his chores slide. So standing there in the kitchen the next afternoon, Mark's dad told him he was grounded. He could not use the car or be out with his friends for the next two weeks.

Mark got angry and tried to explain why he had come in late, but his dad wanted "no excuses." Mark spoke louder and more forcefully in reaction to his dad's "that's final" attitude. Then his dad confronted him, telling him not to raise his voice and asserting that he was irresponsible, selfish, and thinking only of himself. To make his point, he poked Mark in the chest.

"Don't poke me like that!" Mark insisted, and poked back. He was as tall as his dad.

His father became incensed. "Don't you talk to me or touch me like that! Do you hear?!" This was not a question. It was an ultimatum.

"You did it to me!"

"I am your father, and you are under my authority. I'll *poke* you (his finger spiking Mark's chest a second time) if it helps you get the point. You're only going to make things worse for yourself if you keep up this attitude."

Mark raised his hand for a return poke, but his father grabbed his wrist pretty hard. He didn't mean for it to hurt, but as Mark winced and twisted away to free himself, they both fell to the kitchen floor—Mark trying to pull his hand back and his dad trying to immobilize him.

One very long minute later, Mark's dad, outweighing his son by seventy-five pounds, had him pinned on his stomach. "Ok, I give up, just let me go!" Mark appealed.

They got up and Mark stormed out of the kitchen, muttering, "I hate this family. I can't wait to get outta here!"

His father walked into the family room, still breathing hard and thinking that in their case the name of that room was ironic, even contradictory. "Lord, what just happened here?" he sighed in prayer, just under his breath.

Mark certainly did a lot of things wrong in this encounter. But his father helped to move things toward serious conflict as well. His father had the primary responsibility to set and maintain a helpful, peaceful tone for the conversation, and to lead his son by grace. Instead, he asserted his authority and challenged his son by force of personality. In reality, God was nowhere to be found in this conversation. It was a matter of one man against another. No wonder it ended up *mano a mano*.

Mark's dad would have done well to attend to his attitude—his "stance"—before he spoke to his son. He could see Mark's offenses and knew that his irresponsibility and emerging disrespect couldn't go without comment. He had faithful intentions. But because he was not prepared, he just did what "came naturally," setting the stage for an out-of-control, angry confrontation.

It's not enough for me to see my teen's sins and failures. There are things about God's purpose in the overall situation, and things about myself, that I must see as well. I need to enter discussions like the one between Mark and his father with God's goals as my goals. This means looking at both my teen and myself from a solid, honest, biblical perspective. I need to bring the proper biblical stance to these discussions.

Consider the attention professional athletes give to that moment just before they face their event. Imagine Michael Phelps in the 2008 Olympics, coiled in diving position at the head of his racing lane, waiting for the starting gun, seeking that history-making swimming medal. Or a gymnast ready to mount a 4-inch-wide balance beam in front of 100 million television viewers. They know that success will be impossible unless they bring to the very first moment of their event exactly the right mental and physical posture.

Whatever you call it—poise, balance, attitude, perspective, preparation, heart, or something else—it is absolutely critical. We will call it "stance," and the one you bring to your discussions with your angry or disinterested teen can make all the difference.

This chapter and the next will coach you about two features of your stance which will position you to apply effectively the communication process described in the rest of this book.* These two features are *a desire to glorify God*, and *an awareness of your own sinfulness*. Mark's dad did not bring either feature to that unfortunate discussion in the kitchen. But parents who take the right stance are far better able to manage their own temptations to impatience, anger, or self-righteousness, and far better able to lead their teens in ways that are truly constructive.

Focus on God's Glory

Why does your family exist? What is your shared purpose? What actually is the goal of that complex web of interpersonal relationships, obligations, and experiences? Parents of particularly challenging teens may answer these questions by placing too much

*These two features of stance are also emphasized in the work of Ken Sande and Peacemaker Ministries. The excellent book, *The Peacemaker*, develops these and other concepts for biblical conflict resolution.

emphasis on an absence of conflict. But having a goal of "peace at any price" only compounds a family's difficulties.

David and Phyllis York were husband-and-wife psychologists with out-of-control teens. In the last third of the twentieth century they popularized something called the Toughlove movement. Although not writing from a Christian perspective, they asserted that if a parent's primary goal when faced with defiant and angry teens was to create peace and harmony in the home, the parents were courting failure.

It's not hard to see why this is true. When the ideal is a simple absence of conflict, one of three things is likely to happen. Either the parents hand all authority to the teens, making parental standards irrelevant, they use their control of resources to manipulate their teen, or the parents become dictators imposing harsh, legalistic, unbending rules. Not everything about the Toughlove approach is biblical, but on this point the Scriptures agree. For the Christian parent, there is something much more important and far more valuable than peace and tranquility.

This book endorses the perspective that a family's highest purpose, God's greatest goal for us, is to pursue his glory in all of life—including in the parenting of difficult teens.

Throughout the Bible, from Genesis 1 to Revelation 22, one person is center stage—God. He begins things and he ends them. His overarching purpose could not be more clear. He intends for himself to be the center of attention in peoples' lives and priorities. His glory is paramount. This is everywhere evident in Scripture.

- God's revelation begins in Genesis 1:1 with him as its subject. "In the beginning God created the heavens and the earth."
- The first commandment asserts his preeminence in his moral law. "You shall have no other gods before me" (Exodus 1:3).
- The second, third, and fourth commandments seal the obligation to have him as God alone in our actions, words,

and attitudes. "You shall not make for yourself a carved image" (20:4), "You shall not take the name of the Lord your God in vain" (20:7), "Remember the Sabbath day to keep it holy" (20:8).

- The benefits God bestows upon his people are not first of all for our welfare but for his glory. "May God be gracious to us and bless us and make his face to shine upon us, *that your way may be known on earth*, your saving power among all nations. Let the peoples praise you, O God; let all the peoples praise you!" (Psalm 67:1–2, emphasis added). "Help us, O God of our salvation, *for the glory of your name*; deliver us, and atone for our sins, *for your name's sake*! Why should the nations say, "Where is their God?" (Psalm 79:9–10a, emphasis added).

- God affirms that he alone calls and saves his people and gives them "as a covenant for the people, a light for the nations, to open the eyes that are blind, to bring out the prisoners from the dungeon, from the prison those who sit in darkness." Then he asserts the reason for this. "I am the Lord; that is my name; my glory I give to no other, nor my praise to carved idols" (Isaiah 42:6–8).

- God's world-wide mission is to advance his glory. "I will . . . bring my sons from afar and my daughters from the end of the earth, everyone who is called by my name, whom I created for my glory, whom I formed and made" (Isaiah 43:6–7).

- Ezekiel states forty-two times that the reason for the Lord's judgments and mercy is, "That you [Israel, the world, the enemies, his people] may know that I am the Lord" (e.g., Ezekiel 6:10, 13; 12:15–16; 13:9, 21; 28:26; 36:11; 39:28).

- As noted earlier, Paul asserts that God's purpose for believers is to live for God's glory in all that we do, even in our mundane eating and drinking, "So, whether you eat or drink or whatever you do, do all to the glory of God" (1 Corinthians 10:31).

- In the great conclusion to the theological section of Romans, Paul exclaims that God's purpose revolves around his glory. "Oh, the depth of the riches and wisdom and knowledge of God! How unsearchable are his judgments and how inscrutable his ways! 'For who has known the mind of the Lord, or who has been his counselor?' 'Or who has given a gift to him that he might be repaid?' For from him and through him and to him are all things. To him be glory forever. Amen." (Romans 11:33–36).

- Likewise, the celebration in eternity will not be centered around us, but around the Lamb and the One who sits on the throne. "Then I looked, and I heard around the throne and the living creatures and the elders the voice of many angels, numbering myriads of myriads and thousands of thousands, saying with a loud voice, 'Worthy is the Lamb who was slain, to receive power and wealth and wisdom and might and honor and glory and blessing!' And I heard every creature in heaven and on earth and under the earth and in the sea, and all that is in them, saying, 'To him who sits on the throne and to the Lamb be blessing and honor and glory and might forever and ever!' And the four living creatures said, 'Amen!' and the elders fell down and worshiped" (Revelation 5:11–14).

- Because of some of the remarkable spiritual privileges God gave the apostle John, he might have easily missed the point of all of history. But God used his angelic beings to help John keep an accurate focus. "I, John, am the one who heard and saw these things. And when I heard and saw them, I fell down to worship at the feet of the angel who showed them to me, but he said to me, 'You must not do that! I am a fellow servant with you and your brothers the prophets, and with those who keep the words of this book. Worship God'" (Revelation 22:8–9).

- Likewise, Jesus' concluding testimony in Revelation identifies his own all-embracing, center-of-attention identity:

"I am the Alpha and the Omega, the first and the last, the beginning and the end" (22:13).

There are at least five powerful benefits to approaching your teen with a determination to glorify God above all else.

1. Focusing on God's glory will help protect you from fear and intimidation in the face of your teen's threats.

A teen's threats don't need to be spoken to be effective. Most difficult teens are very good at declaring by their attitudes and reactions that "things are not going to be friendly and peaceful around here if you keep trying to control me."

Sometimes, though, things do escalate to where threats such as these three are spoken out loud.

- "I'm leaving here and going to live with Bill's parents. They said they'd take me in. They think you are unreasonable, anyhow."
- "If you do that, I'll kill myself. You can't stop me."
- "If I have to do that every night, I'm going to go live with dad. I'm sick of these stupid rules."

These statements may sound extreme but they are not all that rare, even in Christian households. More commonly, though, parents are intimidated by the silent, unspoken threat. Whatever form threats take, parents may quickly become frightened and humiliated by a child who has become so unmanageable.

Yet parents are called by God to love their teens biblically and work for their good. This leaves no room for remaining frightened, humiliated, or intimidated. Your allegiance to God's glory will affect the way you face any of these attempts at manipulation by your teen.

It comes back to a question we discussed earlier. What is your chief desire? God directs us to want his glory more than a peaceful home, more than our own dignity and reputation at church or in the neighborhood, and more than the confidence that our teen is making wise, healthy choices. Only the pursuit of God's glory will free us so that we do not react with fear—fear that our teens will make good on their spoken or unspoken threats.

God can be glorified in your home situation, regardless of how your teen threatens to behave or actually does behave. Consider Peter's instructions to suffering believers:

> Beloved, do not be surprised at the fiery trial when it comes upon you to test you, as though something strange were happening to you. But rejoice insofar as you share Christ's sufferings, that you may also rejoice and be glad when his glory is revealed. If you are insulted for the name of Christ, you are blessed, because the Spirit of glory and of God rests upon you. But let none of you suffer as a murderer or a thief or an evildoer or as a meddler. Yet if anyone suffers as a Christian, let him not be ashamed, but let him glorify God in that name.
>
> —1 Peter 4:12–16

Angry teen threats do constitute a "fiery trial" for any parent facing them. But Christian parents can recognize that God is bigger than these threats. His purpose to be glorified in your home is not in jeopardy. It may not happen according to the smooth, predictable, tensionless *Leave it to Beaver* way that we dream about when our children first come into our homes. But "The LORD has made everything for its purpose" (Proverbs 16:4a). He is the author and finisher of what goes on in his people's lives, and he is the manager of everything in between. All things will "work together for good" for his people (Romans 8:28) and result in his glory, "for from him and through him and to him are all things. To him be glory forever. Amen" (Romans 11:36).

If our first parental goal is to line up with God's goal of his own glory, we can be confident in the face of our teen's threats, calm in the face of their highly charged emotions, and thoughtful about our words in the face of their harsh language.

2. Focusing on God's glory will give you boldness and courage, should it come time to make difficult decisions.

Some parents must eventually make radical, heartbreaking decisions if they are to pursue God's glory and act in the best interest of their teen. They may have to decide:

- to support a school's decision for their teen not to return
- to allow the law to run its course and not interfere
- to make arrangements for the teen to live elsewhere while he or she makes some decisions
- to have the child placed in a residential facility
- to face the prospect of the teen running away
- to let the teen go live with the other parent, or even on the street

These are excruciating decisions for any parent. For the Christian parent this is doubly true, for our desire is not just for the sake of our teen's experience in this life, but also for his soul. The worst thing that can happen to our teen is not contracting AIDS, or having some other permanently life-altering experience, as tragic as that would be. The worst thing would be losing his own soul.

Our commitment to God's glory means recognizing that we are engaged in a cosmic, spiritual war, not merely an earthy, adolescent conflict. Our war is our Father's war. He equips us for it with spiritual weapons (2 Corinthians 10:4–5) and the defensive and offensive armor of God (Ephesians 6:10–20). Armed with this clear commitment, you can prepare to communicate with your teen with grace, boldness, and confidence. The battle has already been won.

"No wisdom, no understanding, no counsel can avail against the LORD. The horse is made ready for the day of battle, but the victory belongs to the LORD" (Proverbs 21:30–31).

"Why do the nations rage and the peoples plot in vain? The kings of the earth set themselves, and the rulers take counsel together, against the LORD and against his anointed, saying, 'Let us burst their bonds apart and cast away their cords from us.' He who sits in the heavens laughs; the Lord holds them in derision . . . Kiss the Son, lest he be angry, and you perish in the way, for his wrath is quickly kindled. Blessed are all who take refuge in him" (Psalm 2:1–4,12).

3. Focusing on God's glory will clothe you with humility and openness to see your own failures and sins more clearly.

The humble do not promote their own glory. By being committed to God's glory first, our weaknesses present us as people who are just as needy, just as inadequate, just as sinful, and just as much in need of God's grace as our teens. In the next chapter we will examine more thoroughly what biblical humility looks like. Here, we want to recognize the grace that empowers us to be open and honest about our own weakness.

Paul asserts that the display of our weakness really points to God's glorious power because God said " 'My grace is sufficient for you, for my power is made perfect in weakness.' Therefore I will boast all the more gladly of my weaknesses, so that the power of Christ may rest upon me . . . for when I am weak, then I am strong" (2 Corinthians 12:9–10).

The grace to display this kind of humility in the face of disrespectful words, an arrogant spirit, or the defiant choices of an angry teen requires spiritual power that comes only from God. As we seek first God's glory and not our own, we position ourselves to receive this powerful grace. The fruit of this stance will often position us to create a bridge of communication with a fellow sinner—our teen.

4. Focusing on God's glory will energize you with confidence and hope as you continue to live faithfully with other members of your family, your church, and your world.

Having an angry teen can "use up" parents spiritually, emotionally, and psychologically. The draining effect of prolonged tension

Addressing every act...

and conflict can tempt us to neglect our spouse, our other children, and our church friends. It can also wreck our thoughtfulness about ministry to the world. But a truly God-centered consciousness can realign our hearts and minds, and keep us from being seduced and sapped of energy. By not being "seduced," I mean that you don't need to follow up on every single invitation that your teen's temper offers you to address. Again, some parents will be inclined to see this as laziness, condoning sin, or a lack of integrity. But the biblical reality is that we parents have no power in ourselves to change our children. Only God can do that. However bitter or disrespectful your teen may be, the situation is not out of God's control—and it certainly is not within yours!

Addressing every act of disrespect by an angry teen is probably impossible and certainly unwise. In the parable of the prodigal son, the father's own modeling with his son seems to suggest that. Focusing on God's glory, however, is a manageable goal with a promise of setting the stage, our stance, for communicating with our angry teen.

Yes, this book *is* about what to do when you have a deeply troublesome teen; we will discuss that extensively in Part II. But my point here is to allow the supremacy of God and his glory to rule in your heart, freeing you to release to God some—and at times, most—of the provocations presented to you by your teen. This will allow you to maintain your responsibilities to love and serve the other people God has put in your life.

My submission to God's priorities is more important, and more realistic, than my efforts to establish order in my home my way. Pursuing God's glory brings me clear vision. Solomon acknowledges this when he says, "The name of the Lord [YHWH, God's covenant name for his personal relationship with his people] is a strong tower, the righteous man runs into it and is safe" (Proverbs 18:10). Strong towers in ancient cities gave support to warriors, perspective for the battle, and protection against attacks. The "name" of the Lord is a strong tower for us when we run into it—when we trust him, look to him and his purposes, and pursue his goals as our goals.

5. Focusing on God's glory will make your prayers biblical and effective.

Time and again Scripture gives us a model for approaching God in prayer that emphasizes and appeals to the glory of him who hears our prayers. This was how Hezekiah prayed to the Lord regarding Sennacherib's attack against Jerusalem. The general of Sennacherib's army had mocked the Lord, saying God would not be able to deliver Jerusalem any more than the gods of other nations had delivered them. Hezekiah responded by going into the house of the Lord:

> And Hezekiah went up to the house of the LORD and spread it [Sennacherib's challenge] before the LORD. And Hezekiah prayed before the LORD and said: "O LORD the God of Israel, who is enthroned above the cherubim, you are the God, you alone, of all the kingdoms of the earth; you have made heaven and earth. Incline your ear, O LORD, and hear; open your eyes, O LORD, and see; and hear the words of Sennacherib, which he has sent to mock the living God. Truly, O LORD, the kings of Assyria have laid waste the nations and their lands and have cast their gods into the fire, for they were not gods, but the work of men's hands, wood and stone. Therefore they were destroyed. So now, O LORD our God, save us, please, from his hand, that all the kingdoms of the earth may know that you, O LORD, are God alone."
>
> —2 Kings 19:14–19

A miraculous deliverance from Assyria's armies followed. God's word to Hezekiah, through Isaiah the prophet, was that he would deliver Jerusalem, "for my own sake and for the sake of my servant David" (19:34).

God delights when his people display a holy jealousy for his glory. The Lord Jesus taught us to put God's glory at the leading edge of our prayers. "Our Father in heaven, hallowed be your name. Your kingdom come, your will be done, on earth as it is in heaven" (Matthew 6:9–10). In Ephesians 1, Paul repeats this theme of God's glory as the supreme goal toward which God works his saving plan among humankind. He does so "to the praise of his glorious grace" (1:6) and "to the praise of his glory" (1:12, 14). The glory of Christ also becomes Paul's reason behind the great prayer for the Ephesians with which he concludes the first chapter of that letter.

From the example of his people in Scripture, the teaching model of our Savior, and the ministry of Paul the apostle, it's clear that the great theme of God's glory carries much weight with God in our praying. Do you want your angry teen to be submitted to God's good providence and purpose in his life? Ask God to bring this about . . . for his name's sake. Do you want your home to be a testimony of grace, of the power of the gospel to change people? Ask your Father to do this . . . for his glory. Do you want your efforts to reconnect with your angry teen to be successful for his sake, the family's sake, and the testimony of Christ as the true and powerful king? Plead with God to do this "to the praise of the glory of his grace" (Ephesians 1:6, NIV).

What God does in response to these prayers will be according to his good pleasure and, of course, it will be for his own glory. So let us not misunderstand. To believe that God will always do what we ask if we desire it for his glory—even if we are completely sincere in that desire—is to put ourselves in the driver's seat, as if we could manipulate the holy Creator through our prayers. This is not how the Sovereign One operates. We need to pray these prayers, and then (in light of "Your Kingdom come, your will be done") leave it to God to respond as is best. But whatever the outcome, by praying in this way you will be honoring God, subduing your own desire for your glory and your will to be done, and appealing to the Father for his intervention according to the very guidance he's given in his Word. You will be glorifying God and employing the most powerful weapon available for your spiritual warfare as you approach your angry or unmotivated teen.

5

YOUR STANCE

REMEMBER THE LOG
IN YOUR OWN EYE

In the previous chapter, we began to position ourselves for an initial conversation with our teen by consciously making the glory of God the goal of our family. In this chapter we'll refine our stance by examining our own part in our troubled relationship with our teen. This will be hard for many of us. But Jesus taught us that when reconciliation and communication are needed, humility is where the process must begin.

Acknowledge Your Own Sinfulness

So many conflicts are filled with quick judgments. Who's right and who's wrong? Who's at fault? Who could have done something differently? Who left something undone? Whose attitudes are wrong? Who is being judgmental? Critical? Uncooperative? Irresponsible?

If you want a recipe for a big tangled mess of recriminations, bitterness, anger, and misunderstanding, here is one that works every time. Just have both parties bring to the conflict a confidence that they see things clearly and are mostly in the right. Jesus takes this perspective and dashes it to pieces. As you read this probably familiar passage, remember that Jesus is addressing *both* parties in any given dispute.

> Judge not, that you be not judged. For with the judgment you pronounce you will be judged, and with the measure you use it will be measured to you. Why do you see the speck that is in your brother's eye, but do not notice the log that is in your own eye? Or how can you say to your brother, "Let me take the speck out of your eye," when there is the log in your own eye? You hypocrite, first take the log out of your own eye, and then you will see clearly to take the speck out of your brother's eye.
>
> —Matthew 7:1–5

A few pages ago, I explained that peace cannot be our overriding goal, for God's glory must always hold that place. But peace is certainly desirable. God is glorified by peace. Non-Christians get a clearer picture of Christ when his people live in unity (John 17: 23). Peace is a good thing. Yet, in any conflict, peace is simply a by-product of something else: the unity forged by true biblical reconciliation.

In the passage above, Jesus tells us that if we want to move from conflict to a peace born of unity we must begin by acknowledging our own part in the conflict. In his book *The Peacemaker*, Ken Sande explains how, even if you are only 10 percent to blame for a given conflict, Jesus' words from Matthew 7 apply to you as much as if you had been 90 percent to blame. You need to acknowledge 100 percent of your 10 percent.[3] The point of Jesus' teaching is that the first and most important thing for you to realize in any conflict is how your own blindness and sin contributed to the problem. Your willingness to look at your own sin first—before trying to address your teen's sins and failures—will radically affect your parenting stance as you approach your angry teen. There are five ways your personal openness will affect your stance.

1. Acknowledging your own sinfulness can help you take a humble approach, as one sinner speaking to another.
"You are so hypocritical!"

This is a common charge for an angry teen to make against a parent. It often arises when the parent is correcting the teen for a poor choice and the teen is trying to justify himself. The fact is that, while we don't want to admit it, there is nearly always some element of truth to that charge, especially in the broad sense—that we parents aren't everything we know we ought to be. The technical definition of hypocrisy is narrower than that; it involves practicing something you tell others not to do at all. But teens generally mean it in the broad sense. For them, it is shorthand for, "You are always on my case about what I do wrong, but you mess up a lot too." That's a tough charge to deny, but we still try to! Instead of agreeing with that accurate, biblical assessment, we often want to deflect the charge away from ourselves . . . just as our teen is trying to do.

Have you ever said something like this? "My behavior is not what we're here to talk about. Nothing that I do justifies what you are doing." This tactic is guaranteed to fail. But if I take the stance of getting the log out of my own eye, my first reaction when accused of hypocrisy will be different. It may even be shocking to my angry teen, who has come to expect from me what amounts to a more adult, refined version of the same self-centered, self-justifying tactics he uses.

The apostle Paul, when explaining how to resolve conflicts, affirms the need for a humility that is suspicious of one's own heart, rather than confident in one's own basic goodness. "If anyone is caught in a transgression, you who are spiritual should restore him in a spirit of gentleness. Keep watch on yourself, lest you too be tempted" (Galatians 6:1–2). There are several parts to Paul's instruction:

1. The situation at hand involves some kind of transgression. Some boundary has been crossed.

2. A spiritually minded person observes the transgression. He's not a fault-finder or busy-body on the alert for an error to correct. Yet there it is right in front of him. He is obligated to do something about the transgression if he takes his Christian identity seriously.

3. This spiritual person isn't a perfect person. None of those exist, in the family or in the church. Yet this is someone who does care about honoring the Lord with his life.

4. Gentleness or meekness is to characterize the approach of this spiritual person.

5. Gentleness will be fostered by one's alertness to his own weaknesses and vulnerability to pride. He is to "watch" himself as he goes through the loving process of seeking to restore the one who has transgressed.

6. Restoration is the goal. The one who is seeking to help can't control whether that happens or not, but it is his goal. The guidance found in these verses will help him take steps toward achieving it.

In this Galatians passage, as well as in Jesus' guidance about the beam and the speck, we are urged to begin with our sensitivity to the offenses of others and add to it an awareness of our own sins and spiritual neediness. In a similar vein, Luke tells of a notorious woman who, while Jesus was at a Pharisee's home for dinner, was touching Jesus' feet and wiping them with her hair. Simon, the host Pharisee, said to himself, "If this man were a prophet, he would have known who and what sort of woman this is...for she is a sinner" (Luke 7:39).

Jesus then told the story of a money lender who had two debtors. One owed him about a year's earnings and the other about a month's. Jesus asked Simon which of the two would love the money lender the most if he forgave the debt of each. Simon said, "The one, I suppose, for whom he cancelled the larger debt." Jesus agreed.

> Then turning toward the woman he said to Simon, "Do you see this woman? I entered your house; you gave me no water for my feet, but she has wet my feet with her tears and wiped them with her hair. You gave me no kiss, but from the time I came in she has not ceased to kiss my feet. You did not anoint my head with oil, but she has anointed my feet with ointment. Therefore I tell you,

her sins, which are many, are forgiven—for she loved much. But he who is forgiven little, loves little." And he said to her, "Your sins are forgiven."

—Luke 7:44–48

Jesus began this part of the conversation by asking, "Do you see this woman?" His meaning is clear from the next verses. No, Simon had not really seen her. He had seen she was there, and noticed some of her actions, but he had not really seen *her*. Her heart, her motives, and her intentions were a mystery. He was simply reacting to the flat, external features of her life. What skewed his vision? Jesus doesn't leave that to our imagination. "her sins, which are many, are forgiven . . . But he who is forgiven little, loves little." Jesus doesn't whitewash her bad behavior. He acknowledges that *he* sees it and that *she* sees it. But it is Simon's blindness to his own sin that makes him blind to the woman who is really in front of him.

When we approach our teen, our stance must be as one sinner coming to another. As Paul stated in Galatians, we really do need to keep a watch on ourselves. Our conscious, humble, focused alertness to our own sins and weaknesses—our "logs"—will position us to receive God's grace as we seek to help our teen. It will help us see the teen who is really there, not just the angry person on the surface.

2. Acknowledging your own sinfulness will make you a realistic model of how a needy person can admit his failures and move on to make better choices.

When we know someone understands our experience the way we understand our experience, we are open to confide in him and ask for help. The writer of Hebrews makes it clear that Christ is one who understands.

For we do not have a high priest who is unable to sympathize with our weaknesses, but one who in every respect has been tempted as we are, yet without sin. Let us then with confidence draw near to the throne of grace, that we may receive mercy and find grace to help in time of need.

—Hebrews 4:15–16

Jesus was drawn to every type of sin we are drawn to, yet he never sinned. His experience and his identity as the Son of God, one who is our high priest, give us reason to go confidently to him for his help in our needy times. Obviously, we don't have the same blamelessness as Jesus, but we do have the same temptations as our teens. In many cases, although the details may differ, we also have the same kinds of failures. Most importantly, we have received forgiveness, pressed on by the strength God supplies, and gone on to make other choices that God has blessed.

Establishing with our teens that we unquestionably see ourselves as sinners in need of God's grace will make us far more approachable. We must be adults who fully embrace the words of Paul as he acknowledged in Romans 7, "when I want to do right, evil lies close at hand" (7:21). This is so true of his experience that he calls it a "law." As a law, it is not just something that happens occasionally but regularly, predictably, in an almost inescapable, hard-wired kind of way. As with Paul, "the flesh" is part of who we are all the time. It is not *all* of who we are, but it is a very real part of our make-up.

Are you there? Do you accept this undeniable biblical reality about yourself? This is what John has in mind when he indicates that there is never a time that we can say "we have no sin" or that "we have not sinned" (1 John 1:8, 10). Our present and our past are riddled with sin. But that is why verse 9 is so precious to believers: "If we confess our sins, he is faithful and just to forgive us our sins and to cleanse us from all unrighteousness."

Parents who are Christians and understand this teaching don't have to be defensive or self-righteous. They can be confident, even while being open about their failures and sins. They are acceptable to God not because they are sinless, but because of the blood of Christ and his sinlessness, for "the blood of Jesus his Son cleanses us from all sin" (1 John 1:7). This open acknowledgment doesn't excuse your teen's sins any more than it excuses your own. But it may enable you to approach your teen in a way that gives him hope that he can be accepted, flaws and all, by you and by God, and still go on to make better, more mature choices.

3. Acknowledging your own sinfulness will often invite mutual confession by your angry teen.

Some time ago I noticed my son watching a particular program on television. The program seemed somewhat morally questionable so I asked him his perspective about it. When he didn't come back with what sounded like a thoughtful response, I criticized him for watching the show and for his television viewing discernment in general.

Later I realized I had jumped to conclusions about the program. So I went back and asked my son to forgive me. I explained that I was still concerned about his ability to be discerning about what he watched, but that I had been harsh with him and in my judgments about that particular show.

I reiterated and tried to be very clear. I said that I knew that he knew that I loved him, and that I wanted him to develop discernment that would help him, yet in this case I was wrong and had sinfully judged him. Then I asked plainly if he would please forgive me. He said he did, and then asked forgiveness for his own words and thoughts about me in that particular exchange. I forgave him as well. We talked about the situation a little more and then prayed together.

My initial sin in this matter, regarding the TV show, was a kind of misguided moral reflex. I've seen this reflex response more times than I prefer to recall. Because of it I've had to ask forgiveness from my children, my wife, and my students *a lot*. But quite often, thankfully, when I do go back and repent in a genuine attempt to be humble and sincere, more often than not the person I offended not only forgives me, but seeks forgiveness for his or her contribution to the conflict.

Genuine repentance and a request for forgiveness by one party does often bring about repentance and forgiveness on both sides of a conflict. When we humbly admit our own "log," and genuinely sow reconciliation, we often reap peace.

4. Acknowledging your own sinfulness can help you be thoughtful, just, and realistic about actions you need to take or support.

Sin, whether it is committed against us or we commit it ourselves, has a way of stirring up emotions that blind us to what is really going on. The story Jesus told about the woman accused of adultery is a good example. Her accusers demanded she be stoned, but Jesus said, "Let him who is without sin among you, be the first to throw a stone at her" (John 8:7). He was not exonerating her or excusing her behavior. But he was making it clear that the sin of her accusers was blinding them to an accurate view of justice and mercy.

In the parable of the unforgiving servant in Matthew 18, we have another example. Here, a king had a servant who owed him an enormous debt, equal to about twenty year's worth of wages. The servant pleaded for time to repay it, but the king went further and forgave the debt altogether. This forgiven servant, however, then came upon one of his debtors, who owed him about three month's wages. When the man couldn't pay the debt, the king's servant had him thrown into prison, despite his pleas for mercy. The king heard of this unforgiving servant's treatment of his fellow servant and said, " 'You wicked servant! I forgave you all that debt because you pleaded with me. And should not you have had mercy on your fellow servant, as I had mercy on you?' Then the king had him thrown in prison, too" (Matthew 18:21–35).

What led to the one servant's harsh treatment of the other? It was his thoughtlessness about the magnitude of his own forgiven debt. Our alertness to our own sins and failures will position us to assess our teen's offences fairly, with balanced mercy and justice, and to bring appropriate consequences into his life.

5. Acknowledging your own sinfulness can help demonstrate the richness and freedom that comes with Christ's forgiveness and acceptance.

The Galatians were enamored of their own efforts. They approached each other with *self*-confidence. As a result they forfeited their joy, put themselves back on a performance basis for acceptance with God and each other, and distorted the grace of the gospel (Galatians 4:15; 3:3; 1:6–9). To help the Galatians counter these errors, Paul affirmed his own weakness, saying he was "crucified with Christ. It is no longer I who live, but Christ who lives in me. And the life I now live in the flesh I live by faith in the Son of God, who loved me and gave himself for me" (Galatians 2:20). Therefore, he asserted that he would boast only "in the cross of our Lord Jesus Christ, by which the world has been crucified to me, and I to the world" (Galatians 6:14).

Paul, although an apostle, writer of more than a dozen New Testament letters, trail-blazer through Europe and parts of Asia, and an ambassador of Christ before kings and members of Caesar's household, had nothing in his humanity to commend himself to God and make him spiritually acceptable—except the cross of Christ. All his achievements and attainments he considered as "rubbish." His boldness to "press on" was not because he had "already obtained" some advanced state, or was "already perfect." He pressed on "because Christ Jesus has made me his own . . . One thing I do: forgetting what lies behind and straining forward to what lies ahead, I press on toward the goal for the prize of the upward call of God in Christ Jesus" (Philippians 3:8; 11–14).

This is a profound picture of supernatural hope and deeply anchored faith. The testimony of Paul's life obviously differs from yours and mine in scope and depth and drama. But it does not differ in essence. His hope is our hope. The promise made to him is the promise made to us. Our inheritance in Christ is no less miraculous, no less powerful, no less supernatural.

When, like Paul, you position yourself openly before your teen as a sinner, and when you make clear that your reliance is entirely upon the Savior, you can offer hope, for this life and the next, that otherwise simply would not exist. Angry teens often feel frustrated and overwhelmed by their circumstances. But as sinners saved by grace, we can stop relying on ourselves to make everything turn out well. Christ offers fullness and freedom, joy and confidence, that the idols of angry teens cannot give. The sure and certain hope of the gospel, for tomorrow and eternity, can be powerfully communicated to our teens through our expressions of humble reliance on God.

Part I: Summary and Conclusion

Teens who are angry, unmotivated, or disinterested can be reached with sound, biblical counsel if we will simply begin where Scripture begins, and then follow where Scripture leads. To begin where Scripture begins, we must recognize that teens are fundamentally the same as we are. They are image bearers of God who struggle with temptation, some forms of which are particularly pronounced in the teen and young-adult years. But because these young people are recipients of common grace, we can appeal to them on the basis of their inner God-given desires for goodness and truth, the "wise wants" that to some extent reside within everyone. To be both a godly example and to stay true to the biblical teaching on counseling, we then need to approach our teens with two principles firmly established in our own minds and hearts: that we will seek to glorify God, and that we will humbly acknowledge our own sinfulness and failure.

A parent who adopts both of these biblical directives is ready to engage his angry teen. Part II will give you a set of four integrated methods by which to do that. None of this is a guarantee that the teen will respond with humility and graciousness, of course. *Most often they will*, but that is not something we can control. As you seek to glorify God and display genuine humility, however, you will position yourself to see God's blessing in the conflict, to grow personally through it, and to glorify God in it, regardless of your teen's reaction.

LCLP

Nearly all formal counseling and even most helpful conversations tend to include four basic processes. There is *listening* in order to learn about the situation at hand, there is *clarifying* of what is wanted or not wanted, there is *looking* for some kind of solution, and there is *planning* to attain desired changes. In essence, the process set forth in this book is no exception. What is different is the incorporation of a biblical view of fallen man, a biblical perspective on how people change, and a biblical goal of God being glorified and people being reconciled with God and one another. Placing Scripture at the center of the process and tailoring it for use with young people refines the usual pattern of counseling in the following way.

Listen Big—to Build a Bridge to Your Teen

Clarify Narrow—to Expose the Realities
　　　　　　 of Your Teen's Experience

Look Wide—to Discover Your Teen's Solutions

Plan Small—to Support Changes Your Teen Wants

The following four chapters will show you how to use these processes with your angry or unmotivated teen. As a crisp memory device, the letters LCLP can help you move through a conversation in a way that will usually 1) get your teen's attention by showing that you are tuning in to his hurt, frustration, or loss; 2) keep his attention because his interests, and not yours, are the focus of your conversation; and 3) nudge him to change his behavior—externally, and often, by God's grace, internally—because he comes to see that it moves him in directions he wants to go.

These process features should not be seen as distinct stages, like stair steps. They are much more like waves. You do need to see them as *conceptually distinct* so you can give thoughtful attention to each phase of your counseling conversation, but in practice there is a great deal of overlap. When you get to *clarifying narrow*, you don't leave *listening big* behind. The first wave just merges into the second. Similarly, *clarifying narrow* merges with *looking wide*, and that in turn, dovetails with *planning small*. One flows into the other. As a memory device, "LCLP" will keep you aware of where you are and where you are going as you move through your conversation.

One last thought before we begin. These techniques do not represent a surefire solution or a silver bullet! They summarize biblical principles that accurately reflect who we all are as human beings, and can often make a big difference for parents and youth workers who want to help angry teens. But the principles alone have no power to bring lasting change. Only God can do that. Ask your Father to prosper each feature of the LCLP process before, during, and after you engage in it with your teen.

6

LISTEN BIG

BUILD A BRIDGE TO YOUR TEEN

Bridges span gaps and bring people together. Good communication does that too. When a young person thinks his mom or dad or a counselor understands his problem *the way he understands his problem*, the two will connect. "Listening big" or with intensity is the way to do that. It's how a parent can communicate that he understands the frustration, hurt, or disappointment the teen is experiencing—*without* using the words, "I understand." Few angry teens believe anyone can understand their situation; especially adults who say, "I understand." But skillful listening can change that.

Listening is active, not passive, and it is definitely a skill. It bears no resemblance at all to the "listening" that merely involves waiting until it is your turn to talk. Your listening needs to be a big deal all by itself. It needs to get your teen's attention. Listening to angry teens must be big, thoughtful, and purposeful.

Solomon explains why: "The purpose in a man's heart is like deep water, but a man of understanding will draw it out" (Proverbs 20:5). Old Testament scholar Bruce Waltke says that this "deep water" is a metaphor for what is "unfathomable, inaccessible, non-beneficial, and potentially dangerous. . . ." Deep water is that which "competent persons [have the] ability to draw up skillfully to the surface. . . ." One must listen intently to draw out what lies deep below the surface.[4]

In your initial conversation with an angry teen, your job is not to fix, bring salvation, interrogate, or dictate. Your job is to listen big, that you might learn how to draw out that which is deep within. Like the supporting concrete pylons that make a bridge sturdy, there are five "listening pylons" which will enable you to listen big. These equip an adult to build a sturdy bridge to an angry teen.

First Pylon: Listen by Echoing Your Teen's Feelings with Your "Quatements"

"Quatements" are statements that are spoken somewhat like questions. To be effective, they must be sensitive to a teen's thoughts, feelings, fears, disappointments, or frustrations. You don't have to parrot back his exact words; it is probably best if you don't. Translating his feelings into your own quatements, however, can show that you are tuned in to him.

- "So you are frustrated every time you try to talk to the teacher. She won't take any time with you."
- "You can't please your parents—no matter what you do!"
- "I give you the impression that nothing you do is good enough."
- "You get really upset when they laugh at you in gym. You'd like to get even with them."
- "You see that I get upset and angry sometimes too, and you feel like I'm a hypocrite."

The point of listening big is not just so *you* understand what your teen is going through. To plant that first pylon, you need to listen and respond in a way that demonstrates that you really do have a fairly good understanding of *how he understands* a particular situation. (Ironically, without using words such as, "I understand"!) Quatements can help your teen see that you do hear more than just his words, that you are listening to more about him than just his vocabulary. This can be overdone, of course, and quatements can become wooden and sound artificial. But to pepper your early responses with these can send the message that, in your angry teen's estimation, you are "listening for once."

Most angry teens are not accustomed to being approached like this. They are used to being "interrogated"—their interpretation of the way adults talk to them about their behavior. Sometimes they have a point: "Why did you do that?" "Who else was there?" "Didn't you ask anyone first?" "What did you think was going to happen?" "So, what is going to happen now?" "Do you know what this is going to do to your GPA?" "What kind of example do you think you've given to your brother?"

When it comes to angry teens, interrogation may help parents express frustration, but it won't help teens change. Quatements, however, are better than a lot of questions. They form a crucial first pylon for that bridge of understanding.

Second Pylon: Listen for What Your Teen Does <u>Not</u> Want

Teens are usually the most willing to work on areas of their lives where they do *not* want what is currently happening. In these instances, pain is a great motivator. As you listen for these unwanted feelings and experiences, you can plant one more bridge support that says that you understand what your teen is going through.

- "I don't want the teacher to take points off when I don't do it her way."
- "I don't want my parents to split up!"
- "I don't want you always treating me like a little kid!"
- "I don't want to have to go to summer school."
- "I don't want her to yell at me anymore!"

- "I don't want you coming in my room without knocking on the door."
- "I don't want the teacher to keep picking on me."
- "I don't want to feel like I'm going to throw up when I come to school."
- "I don't want you always telling me what I can listen to and not listen to."
- "I don't want my mom to blab my business all over the church."

Any myriad of things can fill in the blank of "I don't want _____!" A parent or counselor's usual response to such comments is to become confrontational. We point out how irrational, inappropriate, or just plain wrong the teen is in clinging to these desires and opinions. We may be right about that. But our goal is not to be right. Our goal is to help, and confrontation at this stage is just not helpful.

Instead of confronting, just keep listening. Make sure you understand clearly what is not wanted. Use quatements to clarify. Do not start probing for causes and explanations. Just keep at it, listening for what he does not want, until *he* thinks you've gotten it. Usually, what he sees and experiences as his problem is all you need to understand for the time being. Once you have built this bridge of understanding and trust, the balance of your time is going to be spent on helping him develop solutions—to get what he does wisely want. Clues to that wise want are embedded in your understanding of what he does *not* want.

You can usually tell that you've made a good connection with your teen when you see a small physical change in his behavior. He may sit up, change the angle at which he is sitting, change his facial expression, become more relaxed, begin to talk more freely, and often begin to make more eye contact. All of these are positive signals. The teen sees that to some degree you are on his wavelength.

Third Pylon: Listen *to* Your Teen's Body Language, and Listen *with* Your Own

It's called "body language" for a very good reason. What we do with body position and facial expression is an important form of communication. One popular Bible teacher has said that we communicate about 5 percent of our meaning with our words and about 38 percent with our tone of voice, but 55 percent with our body language. The wise and truly concerned parent will pay attention to his own unspoken signals, as well as those of his teen. The acrostic R-E-S-O-L-V-E is a way of remembering key points about communication, including body language, while in the midst of counseling. It can help us be aware of what our body language is communicating and the signals our teen is sending us.

R—Relax. Be relaxed as you encounter the teen. Bring a warm facial expression and a comfortable, unhurried approach. Many years ago I worked with an ambulance company. We learned that it's rarely necessary to use the siren and run red lights. There are few true emergencies. You stabilize and transport. A particular situation may seem like an emergency or a crisis to the teen, so we don't want to be casual about the things that trouble him. But we also don't want to be part of the problem by being caught up in the seeming urgency of the moment. In other situations *you* may be far more tempted than your teen to see something as a crisis. At those times, exercise faith in the sovereignty of God, for whom the situation is neither a crisis nor a surprise, and recognize that your peaceful spirit in this moment will help everyone and please God.

E—Enjoy. Enjoy your time with the teen. Allow your demeanor to communicate that you really do enjoy talking and being with him. Again, your verbal welcome and facial expression will speak volumes. Allow lots of laughter in keeping with his sense of humor. You can relax and enjoy this time together because *there is no pressure on you to change the teen.* Later you will put options for change in front of him and remind him of the consequences he's brought on himself by his past choices, but that's not what this time is about. This time is for learning how he sees life. You are there to put him at ease, and to learn—to build a bridge. So enjoy the interaction and watch God's grace at work.

S—Sit at an angle. Don't allow a desk, table, or seating arrangement to look official, authoritative, or confrontational. I have an oval wooden table in my office, with chairs angled around one narrow end. Sitting at an angle gives the teen control over eye contact. She can look or not look at you as she wishes. A table also adds an element of comfort, giving the teen something to lean or write on.

The kind of conversations you are heading for by following this book become highly confrontational for angry teens. But the confrontation is not between the student and the counselor, or the teen and the parent. It is between the young person and herself. You don't want surroundings that make her think you are trying to change her or push her to do something she doesn't want to do. Let the surroundings encourage relaxation and open communication as much as possible.

O—Open stance. This is similar to the "relax" feature. It reminds you not to communicate a closedness with your arms, legs, or distance. Let your body language say that you are open to hear and accept her regardless of what she has on her heart.

L—Lean. Lean forward to show intensity and interest. Lean back to take pressure off or help the young person relax. If he leans forward, do the same. When you mirror or to some degree imitate a young person's posture, it communicates empathy. This is not a hill to die on, but leaning toward the counselee does seem to show intensity and attentiveness. You can lean forward to accent a point, or to emphasize that you are following what they are saying. In the same way, leaning back can lighten the mood when the conversation gets intense for too long a time.

V—Voice. Modulate your voice according to the need of the moment. A vivid picture of being sensitive to the tone and loudness of your voice is in Proverbs 27:14, "Whoever blesses his neighbor with a loud voice, rising early in the morning, will be counted as cursing." Blessing another person is good. Even doing it loudly in public, can be honoring and encouraging. But doing it this way early in the morning—it's out of place. It is likely to be interpreted like a curse. "Leave me alone. Go away. Let me sleep or give me some time to wake up."

Allow your voice, like your posture, to vary with the need of the moment. Be sensitive to the experience of anger, hurt, loss, discouragement, anxiousness, etc. that you meet in your teen.

E—Eye contact. Eye contact can help or hurt, depending on how you use it. On the negative side, don't be obtrusive or pushy with it. This can earn you the "interrogator" label. Most other adults probably have already earned that label in the mind of this teen. On the positive side, communication and interest pour out of our eyes as much as they do from our words or our other body language.

Body language can speak volumes in both directions—*to* the teen *from* you, and *from* the teen *to* you. Try to be aware of what is being "said" by both of you. Be cautious, though, about your interpretations of what your teen may be saying through body language. A girl who is sitting down, tightly hugging herself with crossed arms and legs, may just be cold in the air conditioning. A nervous-looking guy may be more worried about what his dad is going to say about the speeding ticket he got on the way to school than about a failing grade in English. The wise parent pays attention to his own and his teen's body language. They are an important part of the teen's present experience. A parent who does this well will show that he is listening and has some measure of understanding. Body language can help you communicate that you understand it must really be terrible (hurtful, frustrating, annoying, confusing, etc.) to have to put up with what's happening.

Fourth Pylon: Listen to Affirm, Not Necessarily to Agree

Sue: "She is so unreasonable about the way she grades."

Counselor: "To be doing the right thing and not get a fair grade is aggravating."

Sue: "Yes, and it happens all the time. She has these perfectionistic standards for everyone. No one agrees with the way she grades. I just couldn't take it anymore. She's so unreasonable."

Counselor: "You finally got so frustrated that you spoke up about it and that's why she threw you out of class."

In this case the school counselor echoed back to the student what she was saying, along with the feelings of aggravation, anger, and frustration at the "unfairness" of it all. However, he did not necessarily agree with the student's interpretation of the teacher's actions. He simply communicated that he saw how she was experiencing it. Keep in mind that not everything has to be said right now! You will have time to clear up misinterpretations if they occur once you've built your bridge of trust with the young person. This kind of response is not manipulation. It is not being disingenuous or deceptive. The parent or counselor is tuning in to the feelings of the student. The teen may ask directly if you agree that Mrs. Taylor is unfair. In that case, if you think it necessary at the moment, you can clarify your position by adding a brief comment.

Counselor: "Sue, I wasn't in the class, of course, so I don't know what really happened, but it is clear that you sensed that she was unfair and that is what really hurt you. Is that right?"

Sue: "Yes, but you know that she does have her favorites, don't you?"

Counselor: "There is not a teacher in the school, including me, who can't be unfair at one time or another. If you are asking whether Mrs. Taylor can be unfair—certainly. We're all sinners. We all can have blind spots, favorites, and misjudgments at times. This doesn't make it right, and I respect your sense of fairness. Teachers can do wrong things at times, for sure. What I'm hearing from you, though, is that this was really frustrating and even embarrassing to you!"

You are now back to echoing her feelings, tuning in to her experience. What you are learning here will enable you, further down the road, to get her to think about the way she responds when demands seem unreasonable to her. At that point you will help her decide if she wants more of the same consequences that she gets when she becomes outspoken (like being kicked out of class). These features of the counseling process are addressed more thoroughly in the following two chapters.

Again, this echoing back to the teen is not playing word games. There is an important difference between empathizing and patronizing. The effective parent or counselor does want to echo the experience of the teen. This means verbally taking notice of her *experience* of anger, frustration, and the like, not just her words. This is big listening. Genuine concern and attentiveness are what differentiate this from talk that is dishonestly or insincerely patronizing. Again, this is only the *beginning* of your conversation. There is plenty of time for you to clarify that the real issues are the student's responses and not the teacher's behavior.

One rarely has to *know* (as a point of fact) if the teacher, other teens, or the youth group is truly as bad, unfair, unreasonable, irrational, or otherwise off-base as the teen thinks. One only has to *know* (with genuine clarity) how the teen sees it. Most critically, she must believe that you understand her situation the way she understands her situation. In fact, the specifics of the situation in most instances are usually irrelevant for helping the student (cases of physical or sexual abuse, which are outside the scope of this book, are a definite exception to this). One usually can't change the teacher, the parent, the principal, the police, the rules, or the classroom expectations. One usually can't change mom and dad's tense relationship, or the attitudes of your teen's friends about sex, cheating in class, or gossip. The only person any of us can change is ourselves, and the only person the teen can change is herself.

Clarifying this matter of change-ability and change-inability comes later. Right now, listen for what the teen does *not* want. If you start to explain (read "lecture") to the angry young person—by saying things like, "You are probably misunderstanding the teacher's intention," or "He really is a good teacher," or "You are probably overreacting," or "But what does the Bible say about your disrespect?"—you will be in her mind just like the other adults. All those potential points of explanation may be perfectly valid, but timing is critical, and presenting them now will merely ensure that she tunes you out as quickly as she has tuned out all the others.

Fifth Pylon: Listen Until You See the Paradoxes

Teens often lose perspective when they are hurting. It feels to them as if all of life has become wrapped up in this one big ugly problem. You can help them by pointing out the paradoxical fact that despite this problem—so massive in their own eyes—they are still coping with daily life.

A paradox is an apparent contradiction, something that looks like it doesn't fit. The teen is deeply troubled by something, and it seems to be messing up his whole life, yet he is still able to carry on more or less normally. That's a paradox.

"OK, I agree, you did spend that money carelessly, but at other times you've made good decisions with your money." (You can apply the same approach to, "OK, so you lost control of your temper and said some disrespectful things . . . ," or "OK, so you did get blamed for disrupting the class . . . ," or a hundred other situations.) Draw your teen's attention to the remarkable fact that he has done well at other times and is doing all right at the moment. After all, he is talking to you civilly right now. Depict his coping as mature, responsible, unusual, exemplary, or noteworthy. From his perspective, considering how he understands and is experiencing the situation, it really is some or all of these things. Acknowledge what he is doing successfully despite this painful situation. That is the paradox you want to see, so you can make him see it too.

Keep in mind that you are neither approving of nor agreeing with the teen's assessment. Listening for the paradox, though, gives you an opportunity to be positive and to affirm some legitimate choices the teen has been making. This is not what other adults have been communicating to him. Their focus has been on what *they* consider to be the problem—usually what the teen has been doing wrong. But pointing out the paradox shows what the teen has been doing right.

"You feel that your parents are unreasonable with their standards, this school has rules that are nuts, and that you will be grounded for the next month. Yet you still get out of bed and come to school and even do English homework! How do you do that?"

The "How do you do that?" question accentuates your regard for his positive choices. This can be strongly affirmative. You may expand on why this is remarkable by noting, "There are many kids who give up or just become bitter and resentful and do nothing when they face what you are facing. They figure, 'If that's the way you are going to be, then I'm outta here!' at least mentally. But you haven't done that." This may also get the teen thinking that he really does have the ability to make wiser choices than he's made when other difficult situations arise. That is a truth you will be clarifying and affirming later.

"You can't concentrate because of the fighting at home, yet you still can meet with me and carry on an intelligent conversation. In spite of the lack of sleep, the lack of peace at home, and the warfare going on there, you have kept your head. How are you doing that? What are you doing to keep yourself together as much as you do?"

"The rules at school are so demanding and nuts. Yet you come home and don't blow up when we remind you about the chores you have here. How have you managed that kind of self-control here? You are showing some real maturity by that kind of response."

"So you and your mom fight all the time, yet you are in control when you are here at school. How do you do that? You go to work, get home late and do homework, can't seem to please your mother, but still keep your head on straight here and even focus enough to get half of your homework done. This is pretty rare maturity for someone your age. How do you do that?"

When listening for and expressing some measure of big-picture respect, you are affirming some feature of what the teen is doing well in spite of how terrible, how unfair, how awful, or how painful he perceives the situation to be, or how frustrated, how angry, how disrespectful, or how depressed he is. Affirming him is not the same as approving of his foolishness or wrongdoing. By acknowledging and being respectful of this paradox, you are telling him that you "get" how bad the problem is from his perspective.

Genuineness is important here. Be seriously impressed! If you are genuine about your respect, the young adult will usually get the sense that here, finally, is an adult who "has some idea of what I'm going through." Your sincere affirmations, by God's grace, will allow you to build your relational bridge more securely and, in time, give you an entrée into the heart issues your teen needs to explore.

Wrap up: Listen Big

The angry teen wants to change something. Your listening won't solve his problem, but it will build a bridge so he is willing to hear what you have to say. If you try to give advice before the relational bridge is secure, you will probably see the counseling relationship collapse from the teen's disinterest.

Listening big doesn't have to take very long. In some situations one or two sentences will send the message that you "got it." In others, though, you may spend most of the conversation just listening. Don't be in a hurry. Keep planting the five pylons of this chapter until you see evidence that you have made a solid connection with the teen—until he thinks you understand his problem the way he understands it. With those pylons in place, the bridge can be made strong enough to withstand the weight of the challenges you are going to present to him in future interactions.

7

CLARIFY NARROW

EXPOSE THE REALITIES
OF YOUR TEEN'S EXPERIENCE

With your listening pylons secure and a passable bridge in place, you can begin using that bridge for the reason it was built—to help the teen see what is really going on, and what can be done about it. In this chapter you will learn how to shake an angry teen out of his habit of excusing his actions, minimizing his responsibility, or blaming others for his angry choices.

Angry teens often live in a kind of dream world built on deeply unrealistic thinking about the way life *should* work in order to conform to their assumptions and preferences. The fact that they misperceive reality is as obvious to most caring adults as pimples are to a teen, yet to teens, their skewed view is completely reasonable. Your job is to help them narrow down their big, abstract generalizations to realistic proportions, or in some cases abandon them altogether. This is rarely accomplished by asserting that, "You are just being unrealistic!" or "Well, life isn't fair!" What works is to help them use their ability to think and reason to see the hard facts of life that follow from their angry responses.

Angry teens are angry because they *are* getting something they didn't bargain for, or are *not* getting what they were expecting. Consider my encounter with Judy.

Judy stormed into the Guidance Center. "She's so unfair! She takes points off for my geometry homework even when I get the right answers." Judy was angry because her teacher wouldn't accept her method for solving math problems. "I don't understand why she's so picky. I do the problems the way I was taught in my last school and I get the right answer. But that's not good enough for Mrs. Smith. She only wants things done her way. That's not right!"

Judy had just transferred to our school from another school on the other side of the country. I had gotten to know her a little when I helped her schedule her classes.

"She is so unreasonable! My last geometry teacher taught us to do the problems in a different way and I understand it. It makes more sense than the way Mrs. Smith wants us to solve them. But she won't let me do them my way, even though I get the right answers."

"You don't have to do it her way, Judy."

Her eyes widened. "I don't?" she asked.

"No, you can do the problems your way."

Judy paused a few seconds. Then, as though she recognized that there would be a price to pay for doing it her own way, Judy said, "Yeah, but she'll take points off and I want to get a good grade in there."

"Yes," I said, "she probably will take points off."

"But that's not fair. She shouldn't be able to do that."

"Maybe she shouldn't," I hypothesized. "But can you control that?"

"No," Judy admitted.

"So you have a choice. You can do the work the way Mrs. Smith wants it to be done and earn the points, or you can refuse to do it Mrs. Smith's way, get the right answers your way, and still have points taken off."

"But that's not fair!" Judy again asserted.

"So how are you going to change her, Judy?"

"Can't you change her?"

"Me? Change the teacher? Who am I? Teachers are in charge of their own classroom procedures. I have no authority over her teaching. The principal won't make a teacher change his or her teaching methods as long as nothing is really wrong with what she is doing. But, Judy, keep in mind, you don't have to change if you don't want to."

"Yeah, but my grade will go down."

"That's probably true. So, what do you want?"

"I want to do well in the class. To get a good grade."

"That sounds like a pretty mature and wise thing to want. What are your options for getting the grade you want?"

More meekly, she replied, "It sounds like I can get points by doing it her way and earn a stronger grade, or lose points and earn a weaker grade by doing it my own way. But that's not fair!"

"What do you think you want to do? You can do whatever you want." Judy thought about her options.

Judy lived with the fantasy that others, especially authorities in her life, should treat her according to her standard of what is "fair." After all, she'll reason, who doesn't want to be treated fairly?

Reasoning with Judy in ways that make sense to her can administer her a dose of reality that will get her to reconsider her anger and her decisions. In the next chapter we'll help Judy see the reasonableness of the solution she chose so that she will be motivated to follow through, thus getting what she wisely wants. In this chapter, though, we simply want to examine ways to help an angry, fantasy-thinking teen see her situation, and especially her own reactions, more objectively. This will put her in the uncomfortable position of having to confront herself with the options as they really exist. In this way, she can begin adjusting her view of reality in the direction of how life actually works.

Keep in mind that your objective at this point is still to clarify what *your teen wants*, fantasies and all. This is not about what parents, counselors, teachers, police, or youth pastors want. The young person will usually be motivated to make changes, even radical ones, if she sees that it will get her what *she* wants.

There are five realities that potentially need to be clarified in the life of your teen. Not every point from this material will need to be clarified in every case. Some of it will probably already make sense to the teen. But the first one, "wise wants," nearly always needs to be clarified narrowly and affirmed specifically. The remainder of this chapter will address how you can go about clarifying the following five realities for your teen.

1. Wise Wants. As we discussed in chapter 3, beneath the surface of actions and thinking are good desires that God has hardwired into teens. Teens will respond to adults who can identify these. A clear view of them will give the young person the energy to make changes, sometimes radical and rapid changes.

2. The Power of Choosing. Teens have the ability to make real choices which have real outcomes. This is because cause-and-effect is real. Surprisingly, teens do not always make this connection between actions and outcomes.

3. The Pain of Choosing Poorly. Horrible, nasty, hurtful consequences come with foolish choices. Teens often want to minimize these effects. You're not going to let them do that.

4. The Question of Control. In a fallen world, there are things the teen can and cannot control. Some of these things are really bad and are likely to stay that way. Where God grants us a degree of control, that control is real. But even those things that are outside of our control are not outside of God's. Often these truths need to be reemphasized.

5. Relationship with Christ. The teen's relationship with Christ should always be in your crosshairs. The strength of your communication bridge will have much to do with the timing of this conversation.

Let's now take a closer look at each of these areas.

Clarify Wise Wants

After your listening and bridge-building, it's time to bring up the concept of wise wants. Chapter 3 laid the biblical foundation for you to be able to recognize evidence of these good desires in your teen. By this point in counseling your teen, you will have already listened for and echoed back what hurts, frustrates, or angers him—things he doesn't want. Now you can begin to help him determine what he *does* want and from there help him to see where wise wants underlie those desires. Remember, listening and clarifying are like waves that keep rolling one on top of the other. They overlap. Keep listening all the way through this phase of your conversation too. Each time your teen thinks you are listening or that you've clarified or expanded his understanding, you are shoring up the pylons of the bridge of communication and trust.

One good way to discover what a teen wants . . . is to ask! When the communication bridge is in place, and your teen thinks you know what he or she does *not* want, you can just get to the point: "What do you want?" The answer will probably give you what you need to begin digging down to the wise wants. Here are some examples from four of the teens we've already met in this book:

Judy and the teacher with new rules: When Judy came to see me about her teacher's grading policy, she was acting out of her wise wants to be *treated fairly* and to *succeed* in class by doing what seemed to work for her.

Mark and his dad grounding him: Mark wanted to be *respected* by his dad. He wanted the *freedom* to make his own decisions, to be with his *friends*, and to have enough *independence* to operate according to his own timetable. He wanted these things strongly enough to end up in a wrestling match with his dad on the kitchen floor.

John, the "unmotivated" teen who was actually highly motivated: When John and his mother came to see me, I was able to clarify that he was highly motivated. He wanted *independence*, and the *freedom* to make his own decisions and follow his own priorities. He wanted to be *respected* for making his own choices. These were wise wants that lay underneath his defiance, disinterest, and neglect.

Kim and the promise of a Jeep: When Kim wanted to do well in geometry to get a Jeep, she was showing that she knew how to set and pursue a goal, and how to look for help when she sensed that her goal was in jeopardy. She also showed that she had a good sense of cause-and-effect when it came to her school work. She wanted to be *effective* and *successful*.

Some Common Wise Wants

Chapter 3 summarized from the book of Proverbs some of the common wise wants that motivate youth. Young adults:

- want a reputation for trustworthiness and honor
- want their parents to be proud and joyful because of their choices
- want to have healthy friendships, including delightful romance
- want to live with a sense of security and confidence
- want to be useful in the lives of others
- want to be competent and successful in work
- want to earn a good living and be prosperous
- want to have a positive influence in the lives of others
- want to be discerning and thoughtful
- want to use good judgment
- want to be able to respond effectively to others' questions and demands
- want to combat laziness, selfishness, anger, lying, and lust
- want to not be seduced, exploited, deceived, or misled

You can add to this list easily. For example, begin with Proverbs chapter 10 and read just one chapter a day. Ask yourself with each verse or two (nearly all the proverbs are in single or double verse units), "What underlying teen motive is Solomon appealing to with the wise counsel in this verse?" "What do young adults want that would make the counsel in this verse make sense to them?" As we have seen, Proverbs is a parenting-of-young-adults book. Allow the coaching that the writers are doing in Proverbs to help you become a more skillful parent.

Store Up Clues that Point to Wise Wants

Store up clues to your teen's wise wants during the Listen Big aspect of your conversation. Be asking yourself, "What desires lie behind what he *does not want*?" Make mental notes to yourself, which you can put to use once the bridge of communication is in place.

Once that bridge has been built, the way is clear for you to commend what you've noticed about his wise wants. Talk to him in a humble way that asks questions rather than proclaims the existence of the wise wants you think you see in him. This keeps you from being a judge. It lets your teen know that you are listening, are impressed with some positive things, and are not focusing exclusively on his mess-ups, anger, and disrespect.

Keep in mind that doing this does not mean you are ignoring sin, irresponsibility, or disobedience in your teen. You are simply bringing other features of who your teen is to the forefront for discussion. This is likely to be as unsettling for your teen (it's not what usually happens!) as it feels strange to you to approach him or her in this way.

- "Judy, it sounds like you are saying that you really do want to succeed in class. Is that right? You are not just giving up because you sense that you are being treated unfairly. You seem to see the value of being persistent and want to succeed in as effective a way as possible. Am I reading you accurately?"
- "Mark, there are some things that you are showing me by coming in late and even by some of the ways you are living here at home. You want to be your own person, it seems. Is that right? You'd like to operate on a schedule

of your choosing, not one that we set for you as your parents. True? You seem to feel these things very deeply. There is real maturity about those desires, Mark. They are things I want for you too."

- "John, I know your mom thinks you are not very motivated, but I see several things about your choices that are really very commendable. You want to be independent in your choices, don't you? You also have a deep sense of what it means to be committed to a position that you believe in. Is that right? You want to make your own decisions!"

- "Kim, you could have just thrown in the towel when it looked like you wouldn't make the honor roll. In a way, the dream of that Jeep looked like it was fading. But you had the maturity to set a goal and try to aim for it. And you have the stubbornness to really go after the goal you set. You seem to have a good sense that actions have consequences, and you want to do what is necessary to get the results you want. Is that what I'm hearing you say?"

Echo Your Teen's Goal or Wise Want

Clarify this goal by echoing your teen's feelings and desires as you see them.

- "So you are saying that what you really want is the independence to make your own adult choices."
- "So you are saying that you want your mom to think you are mature and can be trusted to be out without her checking on you."
- "You want the kids at school to respect you and not make fun of you."
- "You want your room to be off-limits to anyone unless you invite them in."

Your teen may affirm or correct your understanding of what he wants. Don't be threatened by that. It is initially OK for you to miss the mark here. What's important is that you acknowledge that you missed it and ask him to say again what he really wants out of this situation. Then echo back to him the wise want you think you detect under the surface. Don't try to move on beyond this clarifying point until it seems that both of you have a crystal clear concept of what your teen really does wisely want.

Commend the Wise Want Genuinely

There is growth, maturity, responsibility, and dependability in wanting what is wise. Contrast your teen's wise wants with the foolish wants of some others. Draw attention to the fact that some young people you've known have been content to stumble along and make choices that are self-destructive. Such teens won't take the bold steps or do the serious thinking that will help them get what they truly want. You may even want to use some of your own failed efforts as a reason for why you are commending your teen.

"Tim, I'm not saying that I like all the language and anger you've used today, but I do want you to know that I respect the desire you have to be your own person, to make your own way, and to bear your own load of responsibility without me or others looking over your shoulder all of the time. That is a level of maturity which I have prayed for and hoped to see since you were just a child."

Consider Introducing the Concept of Common Grace

You do not necessarily have to use the term "common grace" to begin to introduce the concept.

"Do you know why you want to have this respect? (Or be successful, or have freedom, or be independent, or honor his folks, or have a close relationship with the opposite sex, etc.) *Because God has put those good desires there. He's built them into us all. You have a case of the 'normals.' God has made life to work that way. He has created you in his image with these desires.* Some of what you have been doing may not be getting you what you want in these areas, but it sounds like what you want is very wise. I respect that."

This kind of encouragement can go a long way in a young person who sees the adult authorities in his life, and maybe even God, as the enemy. Even the most stubbornly antagonistic teen will often warm up to this kind of affirmation. It can do great things for that communication bridge.

Express the Want in Positive Terms

It's tough to aim for a negative goal.

"I don't want all this hassle here at home! I don't want you all over my back!" Tom said.

"I agree. It can seem like I'm all over you, Tom. These are things you *don't* want. I wouldn't want that either. Tell me, though, what you *do* want. I think I am getting what you don't want. You don't want to feel like you can't do anything without me checking on everything you do, like a little kid. I don't think I've tuned in to that very effectively before. But tell me what you do want things to be like."

Tom's response will give you an opportunity to identify wise wants that lie beneath his immediate desires.

Later in this book, when we discuss planning, we will come back to this matter of thinking in terms of positive goals rather than negative ones. You can't really plan to attain negative goals like *not* swearing, *not* getting angry, *not* slamming the door, or *not* coming in late. You will help your teen identify things that he wants *his positive behavior* to actually affect. We'll focus more on these choices in the next chapter, "Looking Wide."

Clarify the Power of Choosing

A teen becomes angry when he wants but believes he is not getting: respect, honor, justice, success, friends, trust, freedom, fairness, peace, a good reputation, healthy relationships, a happy family, approving parents, the privileges to rule, lead, manage, or get things, and much more. These angry teens often do not get what they want because they do not recognize the reality of cause-and-effect.

A Teen's Choices Dictate Cause and Effect

Certain kinds of choices we make tend to bring about predictable responses from others. Adults are often amazed to learn that some teens just don't make these cause-and-effect connections between their behaviors and specific outcomes. In the magical universe of the angry teen, mysterious forces are at work, producing in their lives results that are completely detached from their behavior. The angry teen rarely sees that his attitudes and behaviors (of disrespect, disobedience, filthy language, dishonor, rebellion, defiance, disinterest, laziness, being mouthy, acting out, refusing to cooperate, neglecting homework, etc.) are seriously adding to his losses and blocking what he wants. Instead, he sees others, usually authorities in his life, as the source of his frustrations.

Such teens do not see how their reactions or choices often earn them the opposite of what they truly desire. The LCLP approach, however, can help them "get it." As you help them express their wants in positive terms, and explain how they are forfeiting these wants by their choices, teens will become more open to the possibility of making different choices having the promise of a better outcome.

Conversations that draw clear connections between these two things—your teen's wise wants and the painful things he's experiencing which he doesn't want—will bring him face-to-face with a set of choices he won't like. *You* are not creating these unpleasant choices for him. *Life does that*, simply by functioning as God has designed it to work. The unpleasant choices emerge from the fact that your teen has gotten himself between a rock and a hard place. He can continue to behave as he has done and continue receiving consequences he does not like. Or he can decide to make different choices that have the promise of different outcomes. This is basic cause-and-effect, and it's really all up to him. If you have been patient and built a sturdy bridge of communication, it will bear the weight of this harsh new realism.

Perhaps the most difficult part for your teen will be that this is a completely new kind of confrontation. When confrontation has been part of your conversations with your teen in the past, it has been you, the pastor, the police, the principal, or another authority figure doing the confronting. Things are dramatically different now. You are *not* confronting your teen. He is confronting himself. Is he going to continue to do what he has been doing, producing some pretty nasty results? Or is he going to do what will really give him what he wisely wants? If he wants something different than what he's *getting*, he's going to have to do something different than what he's been *doing*.

Teens raised within the context of a church or Christian school may have a heightened sense of this connection because of their upbringing. But keep in mind that they may also have soured on having it pointed out to them. Angry teens may deeply resent a counselor "preaching" to them by making this connection explicitly. They have heard, "You reap what you sow" applied to their own behavior too many times in an unwise way for that to be a helpful approach now.

Parents can clarify the cause-and-effect relationship of choices and outcomes, however, by drawing their teen's attention to his wise wants and the consequences which he is getting and doesn't want. This usually shows a teen that it's what *he* is doing, not what others are doing to him, that is giving him the pain, restriction, loss, rejection, etc. which he doesn't want. In this way, he will begin to make the cause-and-effect connection without you declaring it to be a fact of life.

- "If you keep doing what you are doing, Bill, is that likely to change your grounding at home? You don't have to change anything. No one can make you change. Other people can make things uncomfortable for you if they think you are out of line, perhaps. But no one can make you change. You are your own person. God has given you the capacity to make choices, wise or foolish. So I'm not trying to change you. I don't have that power. But if *you* don't change, is the situation likely to change? What do you want to happen?"

- "So if you keep on doing (or not doing) your homework in English the way you have, are you likely to get out of ninth grade? You don't have to change anything. But what do you want? Is the way you are handling English homework now going to do it for you?"

Only Your Teen Can Make Different, Better Choices

Affirm the truth that you are not the one bringing the negative consequences into your teen's life. The rules, the dynamics of life, others in authority, or the law may come into play, but his choices are *bringing* them into play. *Be similarly emphatic that he does not have to change.*

To a parent who has been on the receiving end of defiance, vulgarity, and belligerence, it can seem risky to say, "Anthony, you really don't have to change if you don't want to. I can't make you change. That's not what God has equipped me to do. That will have to be your choice." A statement like this can feel like you are giving him a blank check to keep on with his disrespectful and ungodly behavior. But all you are doing is confirming for your teen the way things are. We cannot change our kids at this stage of their lives. They are their own persons. This does not mean that we are helpless in the face of their horrible, angry behavior or language. We must hold them accountable for their choices, and God gives us a variety of options for allowing our teen's sinful choices to bring painful consequences their way. But that is different from assuming that we can change our young adult. He knows, "You can't make me do anything," and you can take a lot of wind out of his sails of resistance by acknowledging this as a limitation.

The reality is that the young adult does not *have* to change if he does not want to. God has created him with the capacity to make choices. He may have to change to get some different outcomes that he really wants. But he is free to *not* change. Stressing these things at this point in the conversation forces the teen into a position he's not encountered very often: he has no one to argue with except himself. "Am I going to change my behavior or keep doing the same things? I can do what I want to do."

Recall Judy, who didn't approve of her teacher's approach to geometry. Judy wanted something different from that class, and had to change to get it. If she continued to follow the problem-solving techniques she had learned in her previous school, she would continue to lose points. She had a choice to make. The school counselor insisted she did not have to change anything if she did not want to. He could not, and wasn't *trying*, to make her change. That was completely up to her, depending upon what she wanted.

Real Choices, Real Outcomes

Sometimes a teen comes to the hopeless conclusion that "it doesn't matter what I do, nothing will change." She's seen failure after failure. In her way of thinking nothing can really make things better at home, at school, or with alienated friends. Usually teens who are this hopeless have lost sight (or have never truly grasped) the connection between their choices and specific outcomes. In these cases, some simple illustrations can give them hope or serve as a quick refresher course in cause-and-effect. This is a time to relax and enjoy your conversation. It can be humorous and still make the important point that your teen is capable of making good decisions that bring good results.

- "This morning when you woke up, did you feel a kind of pressure in your mid-section, get out of bed, go down the hall to a little room, and, shortly thereafter, feel relief?" Typically the young person will laugh and say, "Yeah, I went to the bathroom." Your response can be something like, "That was a good decision. Seriously. You could have just stayed in bed, messed yourself, and lay in it all day. There are people in institutions that do that. You made a good decision!"

- "I notice you have clothes on . . . That is a good decision. We've both read or heard about people who go out in public without their clothes on."
- "Did you drive to school . . . stop at red lights, turn left from left lanes, and keep the doors closed while moving? Those were good decisions."
- "Have you gone to class today? Did you stand up and curse at the teachers? Did you throw a desk out the window or books at the teacher? There are schools where these things happen. You've made good decisions to behave differently."

Change is possible. It occurs because we make different decisions from those we have made in the past. "Marsha, God has created you with the ability to make choices. That comes with being created in his image. Yes, you may have made some bad decisions, even terrible ones. That's OK. I'm going to love you and walk with you through whatever those things may bring upon you. But until you are no longer living on this planet you have the ability to make other choices that can have different outcomes."

Angry teens are not used to being confronted with their own power to choose. They are not used to finding an enemy within. They are used to asserting their own "right" to make decisions or exercise independence, and they are used to fighting anyone who challenges that right. When you assert what they *can* do—instead of telling them what they *can't*—you interrupt a deeply ingrained habit of defensiveness and pull the rug out from under many of their favorite knee-jerk arguments.

This clarification often dramatically pits the teen against himself, instead of against you and others. You cannot change him, you openly acknowledge that, and you are not trying to. Only he can change himself. Telling the truth in this way is powerful. It throws teens off guard, and often causes them to trust and open up to you in new ways.

Clarify the Pain of Choosing Poorly

By now, in talking with your teen, she has expressed some of the pain, loss, hurt, frustration, and disappointment she has faced. Such painful outcomes, or the fear of them, can motivate us to make better choices. This is how God has ordered the world. "If you are wise, your wisdom will reward you. If you are a mocker, you alone will suffer" (Proverbs 9:12, NIV). "Good sense wins favor, but the way of the treacherous is their ruin [marginal reading "is rough"]" (Proverbs 13:15). "Whoever ignores instruction despises himself" (Proverbs 15:32).

Yet often our teens want to deny the severity of the hurts they are feeling, especially if they sense that their own behavior is causing the hurts. Because God has designed pain as a motivator, we must not let that happen. We want to expose as much of the pain, fear, loss, and other negatives they are experiencing as we possibly can. We must be kind and sensitive as we do this, but like a good physician, we need to expose the wound as fully as possible.

Echo How the Pain is Expressed

Be careful not to *tell* your teen how she feels. She's heard adults telling her and interpreting her for as long as she can remember. Comments to your teen such as, "You don't want this to happen!" or "You don't want to do that," can easily elicit a strong reaction. "How do you know what *I* want?" "You don't have any idea how I feel!" Instead, allow her own words and meanings to paint the picture of how she's feeling, the loss she's experiencing, and the pain she's enduring. Echo these back to her in a way that lets her know that you get the message.

"I hate having to stay in here on weekends. I want to be out with my friends. They all think you are treating me like a little kid," Melody said to her mom.

"With these restrictions, Melody, it's easy to think that we're treating you like an immature kid. You don't want to be treated that way. I want you to be able to go out too. God's built that kind of a want into us all—to want to be out with friends and to enjoy their company. None of that is wrong. Can you think of a time when things were different here at home and you were allowed to be with friends or have them in?"

Remember, you've been *listening big* for what Melody does *not* want. Now you are trying to clarify why she feels that way by echoing back some of the reasons she's given for her "pain." You have moved from listening to what your teen *doesn't* want to identifying what she *does* want. As we'll see in the next chapter, this can get her to start thinking hopefully about duplicating past successes.

Remember Mark and his dad? What was the frustration Mark was feeling when he and his dad began their encounter that ended up in a wrestling match? His dad would have been wise to tune in to Mark's feelings, echo them back, and communicate to Mark that, "I've felt some of these same things at times. Maybe not exactly the same way or with the same intensity (for we never duplicate another's loss and pain exactly), but enough to know it's not something I'd enjoy or want to live with either."

Keep Their Pain in Front of Them

Motivation for change can come in both negative and positive varieties—some things we *don't* want to happen and other things we *do*. On the negative side, Melody and Mark want to avoid the unpleasantness, distastefulness, hurt, pain, and threats of loss they have been experiencing. If Mark really does not want the grounding or the athletic ineligibility, he is going to have to do something differently. If Melody really does not want a strained relationship with her mother, she will have to change her behavior. After you clarify cause and effect—that some behavior brings undesirable results, and that's just the way it is—you often need to remind teens, in their own words, just how undesirable those results are.

The kind of changes we want angry teens to make are not easy. It's humbling for them to even try to change, and often involves fighting against powerful habits. It can seem easier to them at times to just stay the way they are and pay the price. So you have to keep before these teens their own words about how the unpleasantness they are getting has been messing everything up. Jesus reiterated on a number of occasions that, "they that are sick need a physician," not the healthy (Mark 2:17). Remind your teen how "sick" he has said he is. Don't minimize the pains and hurts. Shine a light on them. Magnify them to their rightful proportions, as he is experiencing them. And of course, use his own words as much as possible.

Clarify the Questions of Control

Some things are under your teen's exclusive control. Some things are under the exclusive control of other people. Many things are under the control of no one but God. For most angry teens, all these points need to be reemphasized from time to time.

Who Can Change Whom?

When the reality of cause-and-effect is established, and the magnitude of the pain is clear, your teen may be tempted to revert to an earlier position: thinking that it is others who ought to be doing the changing. Faced with a growing clarity that they need to change themselves, they may want to sidestep responsibility for the spot they have gotten themselves into. Both Judy and Mark wanted others to change, so they wouldn't have to. Judy wanted the teacher to accept her method of doing math problems. Mark wanted his dad to let up on some of his restrictions.

But how is that going to happen? The kind of changes angry teens want to see in other people are often quite unrealistic. Moreover, they are generally not the kind of changes one person can force on another, even if that were the right thing to do. Your teen cannot directly control the behavior of others any more than you can directly control his.

In many cases our teens will accept that they cannot change someone, but then they may want us to do it! Judy wanted me to do this with her teacher. "Can't you change her?" she asked. One of the best ways to respond to this is to say, "Judy, let me ask you a question. Who can change you?" She'll be quick to assert that, "No one can change me." Agree with her. Then make the comparison with the person or people she wants *you* to change.

"You want the teacher to change, don't you? How well has your effort to change her thinking worked? It would be nice if I could change people. But, really, there is just one person I can change—me." Usually this kind of reasoning is enough to halt a teen's effort to sidestep personal responsibility.

Things That Will Never Change

Some situations cannot be changed. "You can be in the pool and be wet or you can be out of the pool and be dry, but you cannot be in the pool and be dry." Some conditions just go together, and we won't be able to alter this no matter what we do. King David's sin with Bathsheba was inevitably going to cause a series of painful problems in his family (2 Samuel 12:10ff). This is not to say our kids' troubles are all due to their sins. It is simply to affirm that some situations in this broken world are going to stay broken until the Lord returns or we go to be with him.

"You want your parents to get back together again. That could be a wonderful thing. But is what you are doing in school making that happen?"

"Well, my parents do get together to talk about me and my school situation. It's like the only reason they ever get together anymore."

"So your behavior at school is getting their attention and they talk about you. Is that giving them interest in each other, or just in your behavior?"

"No, I guess it's just making them both mad at me."

"And what is that getting for you?"

"Well, they both have grounded me when I'm with them and are upset with me."

"So, it's not really a happy time when you are with either of them? Is that the way you want things to be for you?"

This is not the way this kind of conversation would always go, of course. But the point to be emphasized in such conversations is that this is a broken world with broken people in it, including us. In the midst of the brokenness, God assures the Christian young person that "nothing can separate him from the love of God in Christ Jesus" (Romans 8:39). In addition, God promises that in the troublesome circumstances of a Christian's life (the context of this promise), he will make "all things work together for good" (Romans 8:28).

Psalm 76:10 is about a time when God's people were being oppressed and exploited. The psalmist writes, "Surely, the wrath of man shall praise you; the remnant of wrath you will put on like a belt." In other words, God even uses human anger to advance his purposes. In the time of the psalmist, belts held up robes and other clothing, just as they do today. So Psalm 76 tells us that God uses the anger, bitterness, and meanness of others as a support of his plan. Nothing surprises him or escapes his caring supervision of his children. The most extreme illustration of God using the wrath of man for his own praise and purpose is the cross. People thought they were cancelling out Christ's message and ministry by crucifying him. But through the crucifixion God's greater plan was perfectly advanced without a moment's diversion. Christian teens who are in tough situations, sometimes because of the anger of others, can be encouraged by this truth. So can Christian parents when they have to confront their own angry but saved teens.

Scripture does not offer the same level of comfort, however, to our unbelieving children. Their vulnerability to this broken world is more acute than our own. Apart from a relationship with Jesus Christ, all anyone can enjoy is the overflow of God's common grace, his general goodness and kindness to all people. But that goodness is what we should be careful to point out to unbelieving teens.

Proverbs 9:12, a verse we've visited several times, tells us that, "If you are wise your wisdom will reward you; if you are a mocker, you alone will suffer" (NIV). God has ordered this world so that those who make choices that are wise by his definition are usually able to enjoy significant degrees of his goodness in their lives. This is a great kindness from God, and such "kindness is meant to lead you to repentance" (Romans 2:4).

But God's promises to unbelievers are limited. They can think (Romans 1:18–21), they can live with a clear conscience (Romans 2:15), and they can experience God's good gifts (Matthew 5:45; Acts 17:25). But unless they come to Christ, they face ultimate judgment for using these blessings to further their own purposes and not God's.

Some external circumstances won't change, regardless of our commitment to live wisely. When you're in a pool, you get wet. When you're in a broken world, you get sinned against and face difficulties and temptations. Yet for the believer, God is at work even in these events. James 1:2–4 says these trials develop character qualities of steadfastness and maturity. Romans 5:3–4 assures us that suffering yields endurance, exemplary character, and hope. Suffering is no fun. But it does hold promise for the believer, both for growth in this life and for God's favor for eternity.

The angry teen, Christian or not, may not be open to much discussion about this. But he can be brought to understand that some things just won't change no matter what we do. For the believer, that doesn't have to be threatening. For the unbeliever, it is grounds for "just doing as well as I can in the situation and hoping for the best."

Clarify the Teen's Relationship to Christ

"Tim, may I change the subject? May I ask you a personal question? How would you describe your relationship to Christ?" Parents and youth leaders can ask this, but it needs to be asked in a way that isn't perceived as a challenge, threat, or accusation. Although I have placed this in the *clarifying* aspect of the process, it may occur at any point, as long as you have built a strong bridge of communication to the angry teen.

The most common response to this question is, "Huh? What do you mean?" Students are often used to thinking of spiritual matters in terms of a decision they've made or something they've done rather than something that God is doing in them as part of an ongoing relationship. Your teen's response will give you two pieces of immediate information: what he thinks his relationship to Christ is, and his degree of openness to talk about it at this point in your conversations. You may or may not be able to talk to him in any depth right now, but this kind of question enables you to test his level of willingness to talk about heart matters.

We don't want to be insensitive to a student's being "fed up" with the "God stuff," of course. We don't want to be another authority using God to browbeat him into obedient submission. In fact, I often precede this question with a comment, "I'd like to ask you a personal question, but if you'd rather that I not get into this just say so and I'll leave it alone. Is that OK?" An angry teen who thinks he's been Bible-bludgeoned all his life would not normally respond well to a question about his relationship to Christ. But usually, by the time I ask such a question, there is enough of a trust basis in our relationship to dilute the tension significantly. True to my word, though, if he says he'd rather not talk about the subject right now, I leave it alone. I'm going to love him and help him all that I am able—at the level at which he allows me.

My prayer will be that, in time, he will see the richness of his wise choices, he will note that the outcomes of those choices are what God designed life to be like, and he will consider his need to submit to Christ and the gospel for all of his life.

Wrap up: Clarify Narrow

You have listened big and built a solid relational bridge with the teen. You have found out what he doesn't want, clarified wise wants as his goal, helped him relate his past choices to the consequences he's had to endure, and yet affirmed his ability to make good decisions. If your conversation has been fruitful, your teen is beginning to confront himself with the need to make some changes if he wants anything other than the pain he has been getting.

A teen who has stayed with you up to this point will now be ready to learn how to avoid what he does not want and to gain what he does want. In the first two phases of the LCLP helping process, *listen big* and *clarify narrow*, you've listened for not-wants and clarified wise wants. Now you are going to "look wide" for solutions embedded in "exceptions." These are choices in your teen's past that have made things different and better for him in circumstances somewhat similar to those he is now facing. Such choices hold the promise of producing different outcomes now and in the future—outcomes that look very much like what he wisely wants.

8

LOOK WIDE

DISCOVER YOUR TEEN'S SOLUTIONS

Emily and her mom, Karen, were referred to me for counseling. Karen was a single mom with three daughters. Emily, fifteen, was out of control, according to her mom. Her disrespect, defiance, profanity, and angry spirit had taken Karen to her wits' end. She had asked the youth pastor to meet with Emily, but apparently that hadn't helped. Emily was no stranger to the Bible. She had been brought up all her life in a sound, Bible-believing church. But she seemed to care very little about the Bible or what God said. Recently, Emily had beaten up her older sister, age seventeen, and regularly picked on her thirteen-year-old sister. She was as big as her mom.

Karen came into the waiting area of my office first. A few minutes later, Emily sauntered in. They didn't speak. Karen sat down and Emily stood looking in the other direction. Anger was written all over her face. She was obviously here against her will. When I greeted them and invited them into my office, Karen came in first and sat at the far end of the oval dining-room type table I have. Emily took a seat as far from her mom and me as possible. Karen tried to smile and be friendly. Emily made no effort at all to be friendly or polite.

I asked Karen, "What brings you here?"

"Emily is physically abusive and verbally abusive with me and her sisters. She has made poor choices in friends and is just out of control—in my face with yelling and cursing."

"How do you see it, Emily?" I asked.

Emily was slouched in her seat, looking down at the floor, trying to look disinterested. She wouldn't look at me. "She just yells and won't listen. She gets loud and yells at everything. She makes up all kinds of rules and doesn't give me any space. She blabs my business all over the neighborhood."

"So what would you like to be different?" I asked

"I'd like her to not yell at me. Not keep me from my friends. Not make every little thing into a big argument," Emily said.

"Karen, what would you like to be different?"

"I'd like her to speak with respect. To not yell and use profanity with me. To not be in my face."

"Emily, when was the last time the two of you were able to talk without yelling; when things went well between the two of you when you talked?"

Emily was thinking. "A couple of weeks ago we talked. She started to yell but then we talked and things ended OK."

"What was that conversation about?" I asked.

"I wanted to be out with my friends and she was making me come in earlier. So we talked about it and she changed and let me have my friends on the porch."

"Is that the way you remember it, Karen?"

"Mostly. I told her to come in and she got upset but then we both calmed down and she explained that it was getting darker earlier. She had a good point I hadn't thought of. So I said she could stay out and have her friends on the porch if she wanted to."

"Were you OK with that, Emily?"

"Yeah," she said, a bit more upbeat.

I asked, "What did you do that helped make that work well, Emily?"

"Well, I didn't get angry or yell."

"Ok, that's what you didn't do, but what *did* you do? You did some things in that conversation that made it work for the two of you."

Emily was now beginning to make more eye contact. "I listened. I spoke calmly and didn't get upset. I explained how I saw things."

"So you listened, spoke calmly, and explained things from your perspective?"

"Yeah."

"And how did that work?"

"Well, Mom didn't get angry. She listened and spoke calmly, too. Then she changed the rule and I could stay out on the porch."

"Karen, did you think this worked well, too?"

"Yes. We were able to talk about it and work out the differences. Emily gave me some information that I really hadn't thought about. So I changed the time she had to be in."

"And Emily, you were OK with that?"

"Yeah."

The Search for Exceptions

The core of this chapter involves searching through your teen's past for "exceptions." The goal is to identify a time when the teen behaved in a way that would seem atypical now, but which resulted in a wise want being met.

Exceptions are Solutions from the Past That Produced Desirable Outcomes

Exceptions are wise choices the teen has made in the past that resulted in the kind of experiences she wants to have now. Among other things, Emily wanted to be able to talk to her mom and get her point across. In the conversation above, she discovered that one way she could do that was to do what worked for her in the past. She could talk instead of yell, and speak respectfully to her mom.

She and her mom agreed: this had worked in the past and had the promise of working to head off future potential conflicts.

In the providence of God, exceptions are a gold mine of solutions to help a young person get what she wisely wants. "After all, it worked in the past, didn't it?"

Exceptions Emerge from God's Providence

Agur, the sage of Proverbs 30, identifies wise choices made by ants, conies, locusts, and lizards (Proverbs 30:24–28). Each of these creatures practice a level of wisdom consistent with the nature God has given them, and they are held up in Scripture as examples for us to follow. Agur, in effect, says, "Use the opportunities (as ants do), places of refuge (as conies do), ability to cooperate (as locusts do), and perseverance (as lizards do) that your creator has given you." His counsel is, "look at the resources God has put in your past and present, and use them to create solutions to the challenges you face now." In Revelation 2:5, Jesus' rebuke to the church of Ephesus ended with his admonition to "Repent and *do the things you did at first.*" What they had wisely done in the past gave them an agenda for the present and the future.

Exceptions Can Be Found in the Teen's Experiences

On many occasions, well-meaning adults may have already tried to point your angry teen in the direction of solutions. Solutions may have been suggested to him on the basis of:

- How much teachers care about the success of their students.
- How much a pastor can help because of his extensive training in the Word of God.
- The providence of God in placing him in his particular family to receive guidance from his particular parents.
- The sufficiency of Scripture to address every problem.
- A counselor who has encountered a similar situation.

Certainly, each of these solutions has validity. But to an angry, bitter, spiritually resentful teen, or one who has "had it up to here with religion," are solutions such as these likely to be welcomed? The sad reality is that clearly explained, graciously communicated scriptural principles will probably have little or no appeal. Nor is it likely to matter who suggests them. Any counsel that sounds like you or God or some other authority is telling your angry teen what he *should* do, is likely to be politely tolerated, if not outright rejected.

In the "porch incident" conversation with Emily and her mom, both were able to learn things that could help them with everyday conflicts. As our discussion continued it was clear that both mother and daughter felt they were being treated with respect in that conversation.

"Karen, what was it that Emily seemed to respond to so well, a couple of weeks ago, when the two of you talked about her friends coming on the porch?"

"Well, I gave her the opportunity to express her opinion without jumping all over her. I tried to listen to her reasoning."

"Did that communicate anything to you, Emily?"

"Yeah, it showed she was respecting me. She listened and didn't just yell at me."

"So when your mom took the time to listen to you and not interrupt you, you felt like she respected you?"

"Yes, and we could have a good conversation because I didn't yell at her, either."

"Karen, what would make it better for you at home?"

"If Emily would talk to me with a normal tone. Would show respect. Not swear at me."

"But I still have all this restriction and punishment for what I did before. She makes everything such a big deal." Emily said.

"Emily, can you control whether your mom will make things into a big deal or not?"

"No. I guess not."

"Can you control whether or not she keeps you locked up at home or whether you can be with your friends?"

"No. Well, maybe a little if she's not punishing me."

"So what can you do that you've already done before that might cause the punishment to end?"

"I could respect her."

"How?"

"By talking in a normal tone and not yelling or swearing."

"Would that be respectful, Karen?"

"Yes."

"Would it be different for each of you?"

Both Emily and her mom said it would be very different.

"So, by talking calmly, not yelling, and by listening when Mom talks you'd be showing respect?"

"I think so," Emily said.

"Would that be respectful, Karen?"

"Yes, definitely that would be respectful."

Both Emily and her mom drew on their past success for guidance in handling current disagreements. They both needed to plan some specific ways to listen and talk to each other for the next few days. More about that will be addressed in the next chapter, "Planning Small." The important point here is to recognize that they got their direction for future respectful talk from a past successful experience, something the Lord, in his providence, allowed them both to enjoy.

Mark's dad (remember the wrestling match in the kitchen?) could have used this approach as well. Mark already knew that things were different at home than they had been in the past. A year earlier he was allowed to be with his friends, had freedom to be out later, and had a good relationship with his dad.

His father could have asked, "What was different then, Mark?"

"Well, you didn't have all these rules."

"That's probably true, Mark. What were you doing then that made me think the rules were not necessary?"

"I don't know. I guess I came in on time, got my homework done more."

"Was it necessary for me to have lots of rules or consequences for nasty or disrespectful speech?"

"No. I guess I was calmer. Maybe more respectful."

"You really were, Mark. That was something your mom and I really appreciated. And we gave you freedom and responsibility to go with it, didn't we? I mean, we don't always handle our differences well. We're sinners too, but we do want to recognize when you are handling life maturely and in God-pleasing ways. Does that make sense?"

The past offers abundant examples of wise choices your teens have made. You can identify many of them by asking your teens to think about a time in the past when the conflict or unpleasantness they are experiencing now was not a problem.

- Has it always been this way between us? (What was different?)
- Are you failing all of your classes? (How are you being successful in the ones you are not failing?)
- Was there ever a time when you and your friends got along better? (What was that time like? What were you doing differently?)
- Was there a time when your mom did trust you? (What were you doing that made her trust you more?)
- Think of a time when the teachers did seem to give you extra help. (How did you approach them so that they were willing to help?)
- When was it different at home between you and me? (What were you doing to make things different then?)
- Has there been a time when we gave you freedom to do something that wasn't exactly what we would choose?

(What were you doing that gave us the message that we could trust you with more freedom at that time?)

Exceptions Can Be Found in Unexpected Places

Sometimes teens can't seem to identify a time when things were different. Keep in mind that you don't need an identical situation to find an exception that suggests a solution. It's the underlying wise choice you want to highlight, regardless of the situational specifics. Focus on the core conflict between what your teen wants and what he or she must overcome to satisfy that want. For example, "Can you think of a time when . . ."

- you did something you didn't want to do, but when you did it there was some benefit that came to you?
- you did something that others didn't like for you to do, but you knew it was the right thing?
- you did something you didn't feel like doing because it allowed you to do other things you did like?
- you talked or acted respectfully to someone, even though you didn't feel respectful toward them?
- you had a problem with someone, and decided to talk to them about it even though you thought it might go badly, but it actually went pretty well?

One school counselor tells of her efforts to find an exception with a high-school junior, Ellen. Ellen was failing most of her subjects. The counselor had to range through much of her life to find an exception in her behavior that could give her hope that she could pass (the desire to pass being her wise want). Ellen was failing because she didn't do homework; she didn't "feel like doing it." Her counselor found out that Ellen was a competitive swimmer. She thought that maybe her training regimen would supply an exception where Ellen was doing what she didn't "feel like doing." It did not. She enjoyed the swimming and the practicing.

"Tell me a little about what you do at home," the counselor asked. "Is there anything you do there that you don't like to do?"

"Sure." Ellen answered quickly. "I don't like doing the dishes and I have to do them every night."

"And you do them?" the counselor asked.

"Yeah, I have to if I want to talk to my friends."

"Wow!" the counselor exclaimed. "How do you do that? You don't feel like doing them yet you do them each night. What do you do to motivate yourself to get them done?"

"Well, I just tell myself that if I get these done quickly, I'll be able to talk to my friends. I know it won't take me that long if I just stay with it."

Her counselor knew that she had something she could use now. Ellen already did something that she didn't feel like doing (the dishes) and that choice paid off for her in the privilege of talking to her friends. When Ellen said she reminded herself that the dishes wouldn't last forever if she would just stay with the job until it was done, she provided her counselor with more material to use.

"I wonder what would happen, Ellen, if you did with English and math homework what you do with the dishes each night. You don't feel like doing dishes, yet you remind yourself that they won't take forever and you'll be able to talk to your friends when the dishes are finished. I wonder what would happen if you said to yourself, "If I do this homework I will pass, not have to go to summer school, and get successfully to my senior year. It won't last forever if I just stay with it for the next forty-five minutes."

"Yeah, that would probably work."

"You do it each night with dishes and it works for you, right?"

"Yeah."

"So it's not really anything you are not already doing. Right?"

"Yeah. I can do that. Maybe it will help me get rid of these bad grades."

How Can I Use Exceptions with My Angry Teen?

So, what's a parent to do? How can you use your teen's exceptions—past successes—to identify a solution that will help the two of you over the angry conflict hurdles that arise?

Ask Your Teen to Think Back

When you have clarified what he does want and the pain or frustration he is now feeling, ask him to think of a time when he was able to get something he wanted and didn't have the frustration he's feeling now. Your goal is to get him to identify some things that *he did* to make a past situation different. Teens will often try to deflect credit for the way things were different in a past situation. You can counter this effectively by "blaming" your teen for what he has done right in the past and not allowing him to give credit to others. The next section will explain this more fully. Here, though, you want to identify what he did to make things work better. His *doings* are your focus. Not the behavior of others, but his past wise choices.

- "When you and your mom were getting along better, how did you talk to her during times when you were having disagreements?"
- "When I didn't have these restrictions on your computer use, it was because I saw you using your time differently. What do you think I saw that was different?"
- "You are passing English even though you failed history, science, and math this grade period. What are you doing in English that is making you successful?"
- "When you started at your last school, you said you made some friends, right? How did you make those friendships? What did you do to get close to kids?"

Profusely "Blame" Your Teen for Making Wise Choices in the Past

Angry teens are accustomed to being blamed, but not in the way you are going to do it now. This is a play on the word "blame." You can use it with your teen. It is one of the ways to talk to your teen that can throw him off balance, so that he is less likely to stereotype your reactions as negativism, criticism, judgmentalism, or authoritarianism. You are listening to him. You have shown him respect for the wise wants he's identified. Now, you can further strengthen the bridge of communication by "accusing" him of doing some things right, "blaming" him for good decisions. You won't allow him to minimize his own responsibility and maturity in making some good choices in the past.

"You can't get away with that, Bill. It's not the way the teacher was teaching that made the difference. It's what you did. You did something different that made you successful in English. Some kids did not pass English, so it's not the teacher. It's what you did. What did *you do* differently in English that made you successful?"

The blame Bill has been accustomed to receive (often rightly assessed by the authorities in his life) has been for his failures, neglect, disobedience, irresponsibility, distrust, and disrespect. Now you are turning the tables on him, using the "blame" word to accentuate what he's done wisely and well. Some common, commendable, "blameworthy" teen qualities include:

- the ability to think
- the ability to make good decisions
- a willingness to persevere under adverse circumstances
- the steadfastness to remain focused when others are distracted
- a commitment to do what is necessary, even if it is not what they prefer

Blaming students for their good decisions and actions, of course, does not say all there is to say about them. We addressed this in chapter 2 by acknowledging that, although a teen's sins must not be ignored indefinitely, there are other features about him to which it is wise and helpful to draw attention. He has made poor choices, to be sure. But "blaming" him as described here does recognize a positive aspect of who he is, by God's common grace.

Students often have mixed reactions to this kind of recognition. They want to hear commendation, of course. We all do. For that reason these compliments can strengthen our rapport with our teen. But teens also see that this commendation, if they accept it, means they have the ability to change. They may quickly see that they are moving toward acceptance of a worldview in which they can no longer blame others for their behavior-based problems. If they accept the "blame" for doing things right, they are also acknowledging their personal responsibility and admitting that they must do something different if they want different outcomes. What others do to them will no longer be the controlling factor. This kind of blaming brings the teen into a clear confrontation with himself. "I'm the one who did well in the past and got good results. If I want good results now, I'm the one who will have to do something wise now, as well."

Reemphasize that Only Different Behavior Will Produce a Different Outcome

One popular definition of insanity is "doing the same thing over and over and expecting a magically different outcome." By that definition, lots of us are certifiably insane. In the repeated conflicts we have with our spouse, our teens, our in-laws, our neighbors, and our church family members, we often approach topics with the same old fruitless and inaccurate arguments, assumptions, and words. Our teens are no different.

One of the most powerful features of the LCLP principles of communication with angry teens is the recognition that the young person *doesn't have to change anything if he doesn't want to.* Continued foolish choices will probably mean continued painful consequences. But the choice is still up to him to do something different or not. Use this idea, almost in a mantra form. "Bill, you don't have to change if you don't want to. You don't have to do anything different. That is your choice. I can't make you change. But if you don't, you need to understand that you will probably continue to bring the same kind of consequences on yourself that you've already said you don't want."

When this idea begins to sink in, even the angry teen will start to see that you are not pressuring him to change. He's got to make that decision for himself. All the energy he has been using to fight you—because of what *you* want him to do—no longer has a target. You aren't pushing him to change anything. But you are pushing him to face himself, his options, and the outcomes connected to them.

One helpful tool parents and counselors have used is the "Coke Machine" illustration. It's simple but gets the point across.

Years ago, when soda was just a quarter, a man walked up to a Coke machine at a gas station. There was only one thing in the machine, Coke. He takes out a quarter (at this point, I usually take out a quarter of my own, as an object lesson), puts it into this big red machine that says "Coke" on it, and pushes the big black button, which also happens to say "Coke."

There is a rumbling in the machine and out drops a bottle of . . . (pause for effect) Coke.

The man takes the bottle, puts it aside and says, "I don't want a Coke, I want a Pepsi."

He then takes out another quarter, puts it in the same machine, and pushes the same button. There is more rumbling and out drops (pause again slightly) a Coke.

This time he takes the bottle, puts it down with some force next to the machine and declares more firmly, "I don't want a Coke, I want a Pepsi!"

He takes out another quarter and puts it in the same machine and pushes the same button. When a Coke comes out, he takes it, slams it down, and angrily asserts, "I don't want a stupid Coke! I want a Pepsi!"

By this time in the story, the teen is usually shaking his head at the guy's ignorance. I ask, "If he wants a Pepsi, what's he going to have to do?"

"He'll have to go to another machine!"

"Right. As long as he keeps doing the same thing, whether he's gentle, slow, happy, or angry, it doesn't matter how he feels, or how he puts the quarter in, or how he pushes the button. He's going to keep getting the same thing."

"You don't have to change anything. You can keep doing what you've been doing (with your schoolwork, with your curfew, with your language, with your attitudes, with your disobedience, etc.). But if you do, is it likely that things are going to change the way you want them to? "

"In the past you _____ (naming an exception from his past, something he has done well that produced a different outcome) and you said it made a difference. Is that true?"

"Yeah."

"One thing's for sure, if you keep doing what you have been doing, is it likely to get you what you want?"

"No. Right now it's getting me grounded (or ineligible, or on probation, or poor grades, etc.). I need to . . . ."

This illustration is particularly helpful in two specific circumstances: When a teen is waffling between making a change or not, and when a teen thinks there is "no point to changing because nothing different will happen, anyway."

"You could be right, Bill. Maybe nothing will change if you change. Can either of us control that?"

"No. That's what I mean."

"But let me ask you this: If you keep doing what you are doing, is it likely to change the way your mom and dad (your teacher, principal, friends, etc.) react?"

"No. Probably not."

"I mean, you can be like the guy at the Coke machine and keep putting quarters in hoping to get a Pepsi, but it hasn't happened yet, has it?"

"No."

"So, what would you like to do? In the past you said you _____ (the exceptional choices he made in the past that worked for him) and it had an effect on things."

This LCLP approach with an angry teen is powerful because it is so highly respectful. Teens pick that up quickly. It affirms their freedom to change *or not*. It asserts their competency to make decisions *if they want to*. It makes use of their ability to think for themselves, *if they are willing to do so*. It acknowledges their uniqueness as individuals and their ability to stand up for what will benefit them regardless of the choices others make, *if they are courageous enough to do so*. This approach allows you to confirm your love for your teen even if he chooses to do something that compounds his hurts, losses, and pain. It affirms his value because he is God's image-bearer and someone God has brought into your life—not because he always makes good choices.

Your parenting goal is to help your angry, unmotivated teen make better choices. You can't do that for him. But you can reason with him and keep his options in front of him with the outcomes, positive and negative, laid out clearly. Reminding him of the need to do something different is a reasonable, persuasive way of doing that.

Allow Resistance to Signal That You May Be Pushing Your Own Solution, Not Your Teen's

Every parent who has tried to communicate with an angry teen has gotten some "push-back." Counselors call this "resistance." The teen isn't buying what you are selling. The signs of resistance sometimes show up when the teen sits back, displays a more closed posture, or exhibits impatience for your conversation to end, either by fidgeting or by rapid, clipped responses like "uh huh," "yeah," or "I know." These may be cues that you've lost some level of your teen's confidence.

In the LCLP approach, there is usually very little resistance or push-back. After all, you are not pushing so there is nothing to push against. Remember the mantra: "You don't have to change . . . I can't make you change . . . but if you don't is anything likely to change for you?"

However, none of us apply these four principles perfectly. So getting some resistance at some point is highly likely. Keep your radar up for it. If you sense that your teen is bucking, lean back (sometimes literally, as we saw when discussing body language), survey what you've been saying, and acknowledge that you have been pushing some of your own plans or goals. You are not being as respectful of him or her as you had planned to be. Repeat the "I'm not trying to change you" theme.

After confessing that you had slipped into the controlling mode once more, and apologizing for it, remind him of what he said he doesn't want: the pain, frustration, etc. Affirm that you don't want him to experience those things either, because you love him. But it is those very desires that drive you to want to make his decisions for him, even though that's a bad idea.

Remind him further of what he does wisely want, competencies you've seen by his choices, and how he's gotten some of what he has wanted in the past by the wise choices *he* has made. Acknowledge the respect you have for his past wise choices and the wise wants he now has. Reaffirm that you can't change anyone except yourself and that he doesn't have to change anything if he doesn't want to. That is completely his decision. You will love him, however he responds.

Don't be in a hurry. Your son's trust, however it was originally lost, wasn't lost overnight and it may take some time to regain it. Make these biblical LCLP principles a standard part of your communications process with all your teens—angry or not. In time, the fruitfulness that often accompanies those who please the Lord may spill over on you too. "When a man's ways please the Lord, he makes even his enemies to be at peace with him" (Proverbs 16:7).

Wrap up: Look Wide

As you *look wide* through the teen's life for exceptions, and draw these to his attention, you accomplish several things.

- You make use of the teen's experiences in a way that can help him . . . without offering "advice" from adults who "don't understand" or are "always telling me what to do."
- You provide practical, wise options to a teen who may feel like anger is the only way to get what he wants.
- You can collaborate with your teen, working together to find solutions, rather than having to be the "expert" with all the answers.
- You can find successful things the teen has done and genuinely commend him for them.
- You can avoid getting preachy about what the teen "should" do.
- You give hope to the teen by pointing out what he's done successfully before.
- You keep the ball in the teen's court without pressuring him to change, because he sees for himself the options, positive and negative.

9

PLAN SMALL

SUPPORT THE CHANGES
YOUR TEEN WANTS

You have listened big to connect with your teen and build a bridge of communication. You have *clarified narrow* to identify his wise wants and some of his unrealistic thinking. You have *looked wide* to uncover exceptions as solutions that he can now practice with hopefulness. Now you are ready to help your teen create a plan that *he* thinks will help him get what *he* wisely wants. If you have used these first three aspects of the LCLP process, a plan will probably seem obvious to you. But it still needs to be specified in concrete terms for your teen.

Small Bites, Not Large Gulps

How do you eat an elephant? One fork-full at a time! Living with an angry teen gives a parent lots of changes to pray for—elephant-size changes. Keep praying. But the plan you help your teen to develop must be incremental. It needs to have a one-fork-full focus.

You can help your teen recognize that change usually occurs in small steps by helping him think it through. This is the same way you've been helping him discover his wise wants, the connection between his choices and consequences, the need to do something different, and his exceptions. It just requires clear thinking. You are going to walk him through a process that will allow him to develop a one-fork-full plan over which he has a genuine sense of ownership. In the past, adults have given your teen the impression that his ideas "probably won't work" or that he "needs to be more realistic." Even worse, he may have felt that adults don't listen to his ideas at all. "They just want me to do what they want me to do!" This time, it's going to be different.

You are going to be satisfied with and totally supportive of a small, simple plan. In most cases it is best if this plan focuses on just one or two areas of change, selected by your teen, for a limited period of time, also determined by your teen. When an angry teen sees that changing one small area of behavior puts him on the path to solving his problems as he defines them, it can sometimes set in motion a wonderful chain reaction. Like falling dominos, one change can lead to another, then another, and on and on. When you *plan small* with your teen, you also send the message that he can make good choices, that you can be pleased by what he does, and that he doesn't have to climb Mount Everest or do the impossible to impress you.

The illustrations below sound exactly like what they are: accounts of frustrated teens who have had angry reactions in the past, but who are no longer dominated by their anger. Their examples are useful because by the time you get to the Plan Small component in your conversation with your teen, there has been a change in his disposition too. He has come to be more like these teens than unlike them. Like them, he is looking for a way to get what he wisely wants.

Teens often think in vague, idealistic, sometimes grandiose categories. But change takes place in the concrete, not in the abstract. This final part of your conversation with your angry teen will draw his thinking into a plan that is feasible, specific, and measureable.

The Plan Must be Feasible, Which Gives Hope

"When grandmother comes up to me and wants to talk while I'm trying to do my homework, I can turn around, listen to her for a couple of minutes, and then ask her if we can talk later so I can get my homework done." This was Tressa's plan. It grew out of an exception in her past, seemed doable to her, and gave her hope.

Grandma liked to talk. She had moved in with Tressa's family during the summer. She didn't seem to be aware that other members of the family had anything to do other than listen to her. Tressa didn't mind this too much in the summertime. But now that school had begun, she was frustrated because these interruptions were keeping her from studying in the way that worked well for her. She was involved in fall sports at school and had a full schedule of classes. She needed to get her work done while she still had the energy to do it at night. Within a few weeks after school began, what had been kind of fun when her grandma first moved in was now an interruption. Tressa was easily irritated and had begun to speak harshly and act disrespectfully to her grandmother to get her to leave her alone. She and her mom had talked about the way she was reacting and Tressa did want to be respectful.

In the past when her little brother had been "a pain," she was able to get him to leave her alone by getting down on the floor with him for a few minutes and playing with him. Then she would explain that she had to do some other things and would play some more later. That worked with him.

"Is there a way you could do that with Grandma?" her mom asked.

"I think so. I could turn around, listen and be interested a couple of minutes and then explain that I had very important homework to do and that we could talk some more after I got my stuff done."

"Does that sound realistic to you, Tressa?"

"Yeah. I did it with Sean when he was younger. I can probably do it with Grandma."

"I do think that would be very respectful and honoring to your grandma and to the Lord."

Tressa loved her grandma and wanted to be respectful to her. This plan helped her avoid being rude and disrespectful, and it displayed honor and kindness to her grandma, which Tressa did wisely want. Her plan grew out of an exception that her mother had uncovered. One day she had asked Tressa if there were times in the past when people had interrupted her and she had handled it better. Because Tressa had been successful in the past with her brother, she had hope that a similar approach could work with her grandma.

Your teen will usually be energized with hopefulness too, as long as the plan of action grows out of the exception you have helped him discover. He will see that it is doable. After all, he's done it before!

The Plan Must be Specific, Which Creates Realism

Again, teens tend to be idealistic and unrealistic in their expectations. Tim was initially angry at his teachers. "They made me go on academic probation and kept me from being eligible for basketball." He soon made the unpleasant connection between his choices and his academic status. But then a conversation with his dad helped him see that what he was doing successfully in his science class could be applied to English and history, which he was failing. This opened up new possibilities of success for him.

This is not rocket science to parents. But it was an eye-opener to Tim. In science he was looking at the teacher, writing down what he was saying, copying what he put on the board, and asking one question or making one comment per day. Doing the same thing in English and history could make a difference! This was a good basic plan. But it needed one more feature.

Tim's dad asked him, "How many times do you want to do these things in one week of history and English classes, Tim?"

"All five days that I have class," he answered.

"What a great goal to shoot for! That will be a bonus if you do it that frequently. I'm sure you'll see some major change in your grade too. From your way of thinking, though, how many days out of five do you think could be a sure thing? What looks the most realistic to you?

"Well, maybe three or four days?"

"Great. Which do you want to set as your goal?"

"Three days," Tim said.

"I think that sounds wise! In English and history, on three days this week, you are going to look at the teachers, take notes, copy what they put on the board, and ask at least one question or make at least one comment in each class—the things that have made you get a better grade in science. Is that right? What a great plan, Tim. I'm really proud of your willingness to do this kind of thinking and come up with this plan. Many young people who have been faced with academic probation become discouraged and just give up. You've not done that. You've faced it and have put a plan together to overcome it."

Here, Tim's dad was doing several things.

- He was affirming Tim's plan for change.
- He was agreeing that Tim's plan has success written all over it, thus showing confidence in Tim's maturity and thoughtfulness about a solution.
- He was letting Tim know that he thought his plan was realistic and that he thought Tim would be successful doing it three out of five days.
- He was giving Tim some room for imperfection. Who among us keeps perfectly to our devotional, diet, and

exercise goals, for example? This could be a good time for such an admission on your part.

- He was allowing Tim to conclude what would be realistic for him to do at this first stage.

Tim's plan was specific. This added big doses of realism and increased the possibility of success. His dad encouraged him and kept reminding him that this was his plan and that he was proud of his decision to make these changes and not give up, as so many others do.

The Plan Must Be Measurable, Which Adds Motivation

"How will you know if you've done this three times this week?" Assisting your teen with his plan means helping him decide how he will know if he is making the changes he wants to make. He wants to *do* something different to *get* something different. How will he know that he is *doing* something different?

Measurability is a form of accountability, and can drive us to action. If we know someone will be checking up on us, or that there is a record of how we are doing, we are typically more alert to fulfill our responsibilities. One counselor friend says we do what others "inspect," not what they "expect."

Measurability Does Not Have To Be Threatening

Planning small includes measurability. But like the rest of this LCLP process, this too must be of the teen's making. Both Tressa's mom and Tim's dad were able to add this element in a non-threatening, unpushy way.

Tressa's mom went on to ask, "How about if you try that approach with your grandmother for a couple of days and then we can talk about it to see if your plan is working for you?" The bridge of communication has been built, and it's Tressa's plan that is in the spotlight, not her mom's. It is likely that this kind of follow-up would be seen as a helpful prod to Tressa. This kind of accountability is intended to be an encouragement, not a threat.

In Tim's case, his dad could ask Tim how he will know how many days he's used his plan. "Well, I could put a check mark in my assignment notebook each class I do these things."

"That's a great idea! Can we talk about it again at the end of the week to see how you did?"

"Yeah, I think that would be OK."

Both parents kept reminding their teens about their wise wants and the exceptions that pointed to their solutions.

Measurability Helps Avoid Generalizations and Negative Plans

"I'll study more." "I'll clean my room." "I'll pay attention more in class." "I won't talk in class." "I won't mouth off at Mom." "I won't watch so much TV." All of these are either abstract or negative goals, which usually don't work. You have to nail down, for example, what "studying more" actually means.

"I'll study more, like I did in biology."

"If I were a fly on the wall in your room watching you study, what would I see you doing differently?"

"Well, I'd concentrate more."

"That could be good, but what would I see you doing that would show me you are concentrating?"

"I'll hold my book up like this (he leans a book up on an angle in front of him) when I'm reading it, or if it's lying down, I'll have a pencil in my hand to take notes."

"That's great. That would be different. Right? It's not what you have been doing. Is that what you're saying?

"Yeah."

"That could make a difference. Is that what you have been doing in English?"

"Yeah. But I also ask myself questions about the characters I read about in English. I could do that when I study biology."

The same is true for cleaning his room, paying attention, being more respectful, obeying his dad, etc. Turn the generalities into specific, doable, observable acts. While there is something to be said for more-general, less-defined efforts ("I'll concentrate more," or "I'll study harder") the teens who really succeed in these areas are the ones who get specific. They focus more intently on the page. They recite information back to themselves. They may write words or phrases several times to plant them in their memories. Angry teens often have no such patterns, or they wouldn't be having the problems they're having in the first place. Be conscious of helping your teen define his plan in terms of changes that can be seen and measured.

Also, be on guard against negative plans.

"I won't talk to my friends during class."

"Well, Bill, that could probably be good, but what will you do?"

"I'll just keep quiet."

"Yes, I see what you're saying, Bill. But if I were a fly on the wall in that classroom, what would I see you doing that will help you actually move toward the goal of passing the class and being eligible for basketball?

"I can answer a question like I did in English class. And I could sit in the front of the class, lean forward, and take notes."

Negatives goals are not bad or wrong. But they are elusive and hard to plan for or apply in specific situations. The only time negative goals are the best approach is when they are constants, universals to be observed essentially at all times. For example, eight of the Ten Commandments are stated in the negative. But your teens need to be able to focus on *specific things* they can do in *specific circumstances* to move them toward their specific wise wants.

Wrap up: Clarify Narrow

Goals of "not talking back to mom," "not sleeping in class," "not spending lots of time instant messaging," and the like, are usually not going to help a young person. Clear, concrete, positive goals are what's needed to produce the changes and outcomes your teen wants. In his exceptions he has discovered specific things he's done in the past that have made a difference. You can help him take this information and create a plan that is small enough but tangible enough to be hopeful, realistic, and desirable. This will make wise, healthy, God-honoring choices more attractive to him.

PART II

SUMMARY AND CONCLUSION

The testimony of Scripture is that our words make a difference: changing people and situations. In fact, Proverbs 18 asserts that our words tend to move things in one of two directions: "Death and life are in the power of the tongue, and those who love it will eat its fruit" (v. 21). Our words to angry or unmotivated teens are no exception. What we speak can encourage or discourage, energize or dishearten. How we speak to our teens and what we say can exasperate and infuriate, or communicate hope and anticipation. Truly, our words tend to influence our hearers toward the most radical of extremes: either death or life.

Of course, we want life for our teens. Proverbs 15:4 tells us how we can help move our teens in that direction, "A gentle tongue is a tree of life." Bracketing the Bible with its appearances in Genesis and Revelation is the ultimate "tree of life." Rightly used, it brings health and healing to broken people. The LCLP process shows you how to bring a gentle tongue to your every conversation with angry, unmotivated young adults, thus pointing them toward life.

Wise, gentle speech can whet your teen's appetite with hope that things in his or her broken world can change for the better. Pray that your Father will use the biblical principles that underlie *listening big, clarifying narrow, looking wide,* and *planning small* to usher in that kind of hope. By God's grace let your words produce, not merely changes in your teen's outward behavior, but, as Part III will show, changes in the heart, wherein lie the "springs of life" (Proverbs 4:23).

HOW TO MAKE
THE CHANGES STICK

Chapter 10
Keep the Conversation Going in the Right Direction

Chapter 11
Point Your Teen to the Cross

INTRODUCTION TO PART III

Jesus spared few words of reproof and rebuke for those who made external behavior their sole focus. In Matthew 23 he called them hypocrites, blind guides, whitewashed tombs, and serpents. Jesus cared about outward behavior, but not to the exclusion of internal motivation. The Scriptures urge attention to both. Psalm 24 summarizes the scope of God's will: "Who shall ascend the hill of the LORD? And who shall stand in his holy place? He who has *clean hands* [external acts] and a *pure heart* [internal motivation], who does not lift up *his soul* [internal] to what is false and does not *swear deceitfully* [external]" (vv. 3–4, emphasis added).

God insists that we give attention to both the inside and the outside. The LCLP features of communication allow us to approach our teens from the outside and then move to the inside as God gives us the opportunity to engage them in heart-centered talk. One huge temptation we must guard against with this approach is to wind down the conversation too soon because of the changes that we see our young adult willing to make. The LCLP approach does often get teens to think and make changes—on the outside. We must not be content with the "outside of the cup and plate," as Jesus explained. Instead we must urge thought and action to "clean the inside of the cup and the plate" (Matthew 23:26). Part III will suggest ways to do this by showing you *how* to take the conversation to the next, deeper level, and *what* to talk about as you move in that direction.

10

KEEP THE CONVERSATION GOING IN THE RIGHT DIRECTION

Some parents are really good at demolition. I certainly have been. After working to build a sturdy bridge of communication to my teen, there have been times when my careless questions have been like explosive charges strapped to the pylons. Instead of continuing to *listen big* for not-wants, *clarify narrow* for wise wants, *look wide* for exceptions, and *plan small* for realistic and hopeful changes, I've found it easy to slip back into my earlier patterns of lecturing or questioning. Teens can be pretty good at tearing things down, as well. Angry teens tend to respond to frustrations by reverting to those same behaviors that brought on their pain in the first place. This can tempt them to lose hope in the entire process.

In other words, parents and teens alike can easily fall back into a problem-centered rather than a solution-centered focus. We can forget what has helped us talk productively, what has shored up our relationship, and what has given us hope. Our shared temptation is to focus on our teen's failures.

Of course, an angry teen's problems never disappear quickly. So with all this tendency to failure seemingly built into us, how do we keep the conversation going, day after day and week after week, in a way that is truly productive and maintains focus on the right things? That's what we will be covering in this chapter.

Your Opening Question is Crucial

In the previous chapter, we saw how Tressa and her mom had identified a way she could respond respectfully to her grandmother, who sometimes wanted to talk to Tressa at inconvenient moments. A few days after Tressa's mom helped her formulate her plan, they had a chance to talk about how she was doing with it.

"What did you do the past few days that seemed to work for you with Grandma, Tressa?"

"Well, the one time I did what we said, Grandma said that was OK and left me alone. But she came back about an hour later and I didn't handle that very well. I was frustrated and told her I had work to do and couldn't talk now and to please leave me alone."

"So you did talk to her the way you planned the first time?"

"Yeah. And that worked OK. Grandma left me to work for an hour. But then I blew it."

"But when you put your plan into action it worked. Right?"

"Yes. It did. I just have to remember to do it more," Tressa said.

"What you did, Tressa, was very respectful and honoring to your grandmother. I know that is pleasing to the Lord. How many times did you do that the week before you worked out a plan?"

"Well, none really. I didn't know what to do."

"So you made some positive movement, right? Something that was really pleasing to the Lord."

"Yeah, but what about the other time? That wasn't so good."

"That's true, but you did make a good beginning. Can you do more of that over the next three days or so?"

"Yes. I think so."

"I mean, you were successful earlier with your brother and one time with your grandmother, right?

"I can do this more."

"When you have sinned, how does the Lord want you to handle that?" her mom asked.

From that point on in the conversation, Tressa and her mom were able to talk about asking forgiveness from both the Lord and her grandmother.

Not all conversations will necessarily go this easily. But the point of the illustration is the way in which Tressa's mom began her follow-up conversation with her daughter. *Mom's focus was on what Tressa did well.* She emphasized what had worked, not what had gone wrong. Mom clearly did not ignore Tressa's failures, but they were not what she chose to talk about at the beginning.

Our temptation, and here I am speaking of both parents and teens, is to be problem-centered in our follow-up discussions. When our teens only partially follow-through with the plan they developed and slip back into their former patterns, that's what they expect us to see—where they blew it. In the past, that breakdown is what we or other adults in their lives have usually drawn their attention to. Their strong temptation, like ours when our weaknesses or failures are pointed out, is to cover up their errors or excuse themselves with defensive and often angry words. That's the way both adults and teens have handled these follow-up conversations in the past. Our opening questions have often encouraged this self-defeating approach by emphasizing points of failure.

Therefore, the opening question of these follow-up conversations is absolutely crucial in setting the tone and direction of the conversation. Left to our own devices, the questions we would typically ask would open the door wide to a primary focus on problems, failures, and sin.

Avoid these kinds of questions: "How did things go today with your friends?" "What has happened this past week between you and your teachers?" "Have you made any changes this week?" "Did things go any better this week in school?" "Did you get to put into practice any of the plan you came up with the last time we talked?" Questions like these may sound harmless enough, and they certainly come naturally. But such questions are itching for negative responses. This is especially true if the young adult has recently experienced a difficult encounter, an aggravating set of circumstances, or anything at all like what led to the two of you having these conversations in the first place. When it comes to angry teens involved in the LCLP process, you should avoid questions like these. The problem lies in the phrasing. Such questions will tempt a young person to think in terms of the problem and "how bad things are." They divert a teen's attention away from the solution he wanted to implement, and away from what went well when he did put his plan into action.

With teens who have been angry, we need to ask a different set of questions. These are questions that invite them to think differently about us, about themselves, and about how to get what they wisely want. We can ask questions that spawn hopefulness and put criticism and a sense of failure—whether ours or theirs—in the background.

Stay Focused on Exceptions and Solutions

Questions that are phrased positively focus on the value and the promise of the teen's plan, not the challenges and difficulties of the teen's problems. With just a small shift in your thinking, you can ask questions that encourage hopefulness, like the counselor who met with Sam about his school experiences.

"What went well this week in English class, Sam?"

"Well, I didn't do my homework each night the way we talked about last week."

"You were going to start your homework thirty minutes after you got home from school the way you said you did it last year in biology and math, and only go out skating after dinner until dark, right?"

"Yeah, that's what we said. But I only did that on Tuesday after we met and Wednesday."

"You did it twice?"

"Yes."

"And how many times did you do it the week before?"

"None."

"And the week before that?"

"None."

"Wow! So you had a 200 percent increase in just one week! Did you notice any differences on the next day in school after you did the homework the day before?"

"Yeah. I had my English done and could turn it in on time those two days."

"That's great, Sam. Did the teacher notice anything different?"

"Well, as a matter of fact, on the second day she actually said it was good to see how responsible I was being."

"And how did that make you feel?"

"Really good. I wasn't embarrassed the way I usually would be when I was one of the only ones without my work being done."

"So, by doing English earlier while you are more alert and before you go out with your friends, like you did for biology and math, you actually saw some pretty neat results. Is that what you are saying?"

"Yes, but I only did it twice."

"Yes, I heard that. You improved by doing something different two times in English that has worked in other subjects. That's twice as much as you did the weeks before, right?"

"Yes."

The counselor then went on to reinforce the value of the exception, the choice Sam had used in the other classes that worked for him.

"Sam, you don't have to change anything, as you know. You may keep on doing what you've been doing and go out with your friends right after school and forget the homework, if you want to. You know that, right?" Sam nods in agreement. "Do you remember what you told me you didn't like about not getting your homework in?"

The counselor was referring to some of Sam's earlier comments about being grounded, embarrassed in class, and laughed at by his brother. He reviewed those experiences vividly. He didn't allow Sam to forget what he did not want, because Sam will only change if he wants to. His failures are occasions to remind him that he has made some good choices, and that he can continue to do that if he wants to. His failures are an occasion to re-teach the reality of choices and consequences.

Sam has done some things well this week. Not much, but some things. Such changes are the first glimmerings of actual solutions to Sam's academic failure. Part of him would like nothing more than to wallow in his failure. That would give him another sinfully pleasant opportunity to blame his parents, the teacher, his learning disability, or his brother. But the counselor won't allow him to go there. He redirects Sam to think about what he did wisely and what the fruit of that choice looked like.

Sam has some goals, wise wants that include getting his English homework done. What he did well in the past week is a door to the surprise kind of "blaming" that we mentioned in chapter 7. He has made some good changes and enjoyed some fruit from them.

In your follow-up conversations, ask questions that focus on solutions and exceptions and the fruit that grows out of them. "What did you do this week, (today, over the last couple of days) that made things work better for you? What went well for you this week? What did you do to make that happen?"

When Nothing Seems To Go Well

Jen lived with her grandparents. Her single-parent mom had died a year earlier and she had no contact with her dad. Jen and I had met once before to talk about her relationship with her grandfather. "He makes me so mad!" The Lord gave us a good connection and Jen put a plan together to help her with her granddad. I saw her several days later and asked what was going well with her. How was her plan helping with her granddad?

"It's going horrible. Everything is horrible! I hate this life."

"Everything has been terrible?" I asked.

"Yes. I started to do some of the things we talked about but this whole week was bad."

"What was the absolute worst thing that happened?"

"That's easy. It was English class the other day."

Jen went on to tell about an English assignment that the teacher had given the class. They were instructed to write a letter of appreciation and love to their mother or father as a Christmas present. My heart broke for Jen as she told this and then began weeping.

"I tried to write something, but after a few minutes I just started to cry and ran out of the room. I was so mad! It was horrible."

"That was horrible, Jen. Did you go to school the rest of the week?"

"Yes, but I hated it."

"You must have done some things that helped you through that day and the rest of the week. That's pretty amazing to me, considering the hurt that was stirred up again in class. What did you do that helped you concentrate on your work and stay in school? What worked for you even though this hurt so bad?"

This was truly a heart-wrenching time for both of us—more so for her, of course. But the point of this is to emphasize how to find some wise acts, some exceptional behaviors that a teen has performed even when "everything" has been bad. The fact is that, no matter how badly the week went, there were some things that went better than other things. Your job is to focus your teen on the things that went *better*. This gives you the opportunity to see how she has managed better with these *other things*. "What have you done that made things better than the worst part of the week?"

Follow-up conversations are great opportunities to keep your relationship going well. As your connection strengthens, you will be able to talk about your teen's struggles on a more and more personal level. At all times, however, remember to keep the conversation focused on solutions and exceptions. By accentuating what your teen has done well in spite of his challenges, you can avoid the natural tendency for your conversation to drift toward a focus on problems. Taking this approach with a young adult who has been angry or disinterested can open up a depth of communication that may be new territory for both of you. Your ultimate goal is to move to the most serious topic of all—the gospel. This is the theme to which we turn our attention in the next and final chapter of this book.

11

POINT YOUR TEEN TO THE CROSS

How permanent do we want change to be in our young adults? My African-American son, Ben, has been designing clothes for the past year and a half. He hopes to start a company producing a line of urban fashion, art-decorated shirts, pants, and hats as a means of outreach to urban cultures. He's learned about different kinds of fabric, stitches, ink, and paint so that the designs he creates don't wash out. He's still learning and it is exciting to see his dedication. I bought a really terrific looking white T-shirt bearing one of his custom designs. It was beautiful and I was proud to wear it. But on a family day at Ocean City, New Jersey, while we were on the boardwalk, I got a small spot of pizza sauce on the shirt. Sure that the ink had set well, I splashed some water on it and began to rub. To my disappointment and Ben's surprise, the beautiful design began to bleed. That small section of the design lost some of its sharpness and the fabric around it lost its stark white contrast. The ink hadn't set as we had expected!

Getting the Ink to Set

Something similar happens to any of us when we want the ink of God's character to mark us permanently, but we have not been captivated by the cross of Christ. Many professing Christians, including many young adults in evangelical churches today (according to survey specialist George Barna), have lives that look remarkably like those of the unbelieving community around us. They profess to believe in a gospel that is significantly different from the world's belief system, yet their lives are tragically similar to the lives of those who hold no such profession. Spiritual power is lacking. The ink has run and the boundaries have become blurred. The Christ-like character that God wills for his people has lost its defining edge. The resulting image looks remarkably like the spiritually complacent and politically correct culture of the secular world.

How can we prevent this in the lives of our teens? The answer is the cross. The cross is the power of God that will set the ink of a young person's character permanently. The cross changes more than simply one's outward behavior. Paul asserts that "the word of the cross is folly to those who are perishing, but to us who are being saved it is the power of God" (1 Corinthians 1:18). The cross is more than a symbol for a gospel presentation. It is certainly more than a design for a piece of jewelry. Paul says that a right view of the cross is to recognize it as the "power of God" for those of us being saved. The cross is God's statement that anyone who is separated from him can be brought near through the death of Christ.

In 1 Corinthians 2, Paul teaches that the life of a Christian is to revolve around the crucified Savior, and indeed this lesson was the focus and passion of Paul's entire ministry. "For I decided to know nothing among you except Jesus Christ and him crucified" (v. 2). Paul wasn't interested in the academic degrees, athletic prowess, artistic creativity, or leadership abilities of his hearers. He wanted their attention to center on Christ, that the power of Jesus' crucifixion and resurrection might radically reform how they think, speak, and live. When I acknowledge myself to be embedded in the crucified Christ, the wickedness of my self-centeredness is unmasked by his love, God's judgment against me is removed by his sacrifice, the promise of life and adoption into his family is guaranteed to me by his Father, and the possibility of the character of Christ is reproduced in me by his Spirit—permanently.

Each of us has a sense that we ought to be more than what we see when we look in the mirror or survey our own lives. Yet, for as long as man has walked the earth, the world's efforts to bridge this gap have universally failed. Romans 8 tells us why; it describes us and our world as being in "bondage to decay" (v. 21). No one has to tell us that everyone and everything wears out, breaks, fails, rusts, or fades. We are part of a world that is "groaning" for the fullness of God and his character that we were created to exhibit (v. 22). Something in all of us knows that life isn't the way it should be. We want more. But neither education, health, self-esteem, economic prosperity, nor having the right politician in office will create the lasting sense of wholeness that we want and which God has created us to exhibit. Neither will any of the hundreds of other spiritual, mystical, psychological, or practical prescriptions for balance, well-being, or happiness. Paul declares the unchanging truth of God to the entire creation when he tells the Galatians that wholeness and irreversible change is possible only in the cross. "Far be it from me" he says, "to boast except in the cross of our Lord Jesus Christ, by which the world has been crucified to me and I to the world" (Galatians 6:14).

Obstacles on Our Teens' Path to the Cross

Jesus made it clear that the gospel message doesn't stop with changing someone's external behavior. In fact, he saved some of his sharpest criticism for those religious leaders who put more emphasis on the "outside of the cup" than the inside (Matthew 23:13ff). All through the Old Testament, God condemned the same hypocrisy. In addition to large segments of the Major Prophets—Isaiah, Jeremiah, and Ezekiel, the Minor Prophets—Joel, Amos, and Malachi are almost totally given over to unmasking this hypocrisy.

This doesn't mean external behavior is unimportant. To the contrary, godly outward behavior is vital, yet it is only pleasing to God if it flows from an internal change. God wants the renewed hearts of his people to inform and mold our external character and motives.

> I appeal to you therefore, brothers, by the mercies of God, to present your bodies [the external] as a living sacrifice, holy and acceptable to God, which is your spiritual worship. Do not be conformed to this world, but be transformed by the renewal of your mind [the internal], that by testing you may discern what is the will of God, what is good and acceptable and perfect.
>
> —Romans 12:1–2

As noted earlier, much has been published to assist parents and youth workers who have a good relationship with their teens and want to help them think biblically about values and choices. This book does not attempt to review or summarize that helpful material. The focus here has been on how to engage young people in biblically wise conversations that will create and preserve a bridge of communication—communication of a kind that has proven to be especially helpful for reaching angry, unmotivated, or disinterested teens with biblical counsel. Once a parent or youth counselor has bridged the communication gap with the teen, and has gained the teen's trust, he can generally use God's Word to talk openly about the things with which the young person is wrestling. This is where other sound biblical resources will be useful.

Before we finish this book, however, you need to be aware that the strengths of the LCLP approach can also become its weaknesses. The ultimate goal of everything we have discussed is to lead the young person either to an initial understanding of the cross or to a deeper understanding of the cross. If you are genuinely interested in the welfare of your young adult, the cross must be your final goal. Therefore, missing the cross is the final danger. But forewarned is forearmed. If you keep the following four obstacles in mind, it will be far easier to avoid them.

The False Assurance of Rapid Results

The model of youth counseling summarized in this book often produces rapid results. Teens are motivated to do the things that will get them what they want. If you've helped them see their wise wants, they often make impressive decisions to obtain those wants. With the LCLP approach, teens who have been uncooperative, uninterested, and unwilling to talk about serious personal things often change significantly for the better.

Before too long, they often become cooperative and open in ways they may have never been before. This in itself can feel like success to the parent or counselor. But we must not become satisfied with the external changes our teen makes. The storm of their emotions may have passed. Their anger or complacency may have been substantially mitigated. This can make it seem like the emergency is behind you. There can be such a sense of relief, because the battle appears to be over, that you may be tempted to declare victory and stop moving forward.

But this is exactly the time when you must use that communication bridge to begin to talk about your teen's heart and to move toward a discussion regarding the place of the cross in his life. Otherwise you would be like a surgeon who makes sure all the preparation for surgery is complete, and then sends the patient home! The preparation is obviously vital, but nothing truly helpful has taken place until the surgery is finished. From the very beginning of your bridge-building, when you are *listening big*, you should be praying and planning for the time you can speak to your young adult about his need for knowing Christ, that unique and all-important relationship that brings spiritual power and faith for every aspect of life.

The Snare of an Exclusively External Focus

Much of the approach to youth in Proverbs, which this book has tried to follow, urges external change and shows how such change is both possible and profitable. Such a focus, however, can quickly degenerate into moralism. Moralism is a belief that living a rule-centered life makes me a better person and may even get God's favorable attention.

In that sense, moralism is closely associated with the strong tendency to legalism dwelling within each of us. At its root, legalism says that God will accept us as his own, or bless us (as we define blessing) because of our moral behavior. This is the exact opposite of the gospel. Our acceptance is by God's grace alone through faith in Christ alone. These are heart matters that have transformational effects on everyone who trusts him. Believers become "a new creation" (2 Corinthians 5:17). Their progress in the Christian life is inexorably tied to their dependence upon Christ. "I have been crucified with Christ. It is no longer I who live, but Christ who lives in me. And the life I now live in the flesh, I live by faith in the Son of God who loved me and gave himself for me" (Galatians 2:20).

Our parenting and biblical youth counseling task is not to get kids simply to act right. Of course we want our young people to be moral, but morality by itself is not the issue. By the same token, a lack of morality in angry teens is not by itself the problem. The real problem is the presence or absence of a relationship with Jesus Christ.

The Illusion of Self-Sufficiency

The LCLP pattern of communication described in this book can bring genuine hope. But if you are not clear with your angry teen that this hope is based in Christ, it will become a hope that is false and ultimately self-reliant. "After all, these are changes *I* am making. *I* have done some of this before and *I* can do it again."

Our teen's heart, like our own, can twist any good thing into an occasion for pride and self-sufficiency. Paul expressed concern that the Corinthian believers could be enamored with a false gospel, a false Christ, and even affected by a false spirit (2 Corinthians 11:3–4). Jesus warned about building one's house on the sandy foundation of an empty profession, one void of living and practicing his teachings. He invited people, instead, to build with a lifestyle of obedience from the heart upon the rock of his Word (Matthew 7:24–27).

Solomon, too, warned young people that "there is a way that seems right to a man, but its end is the way to death" (Proverbs

14:12). The psalmist repeatedly warns about the hollowness of trusting in our own resources. "Those of low estate are but a breath; those of high estate are a delusion; in the balances they go up; they are together lighter than a breath" (Psalm 62:9). But there is One in whom we can trust perfectly. "Some trust in chariots and some in horses, but we trust in the name of the LORD our God" (Psalm 20:7). Jesus made it plain that the truth of his gospel sets people free (John 8:32). Likewise he prayed that the Father would sanctify [change] his people by his Word of Truth (John 17:17).

All of this is to assert that hope in anyone or anything other than God, through Christ, is vain. When your teen makes wise (that is, biblically principled) choices, and sees fruit from those choices, this brings fresh hope. But such hope is limited to the young person's physical and social life. It does not extend to his spiritual life. Paul warns the Galatians not to place their hope in a combination of trust in Christ *plus* their own good works. "O foolish Galatians!" he tells them, "Who has bewitched you? It was before your eyes that Jesus Christ was publicly portrayed as crucified . . . Are you so foolish? Having begun by the Spirit are you now being perfected by the flesh?" (Galatians 3:1, 3). Paul points them back to the crucified Savior and away from any shred of dependence upon themselves.

Parents and youth workers can and should encourage teens with the usual positive, material, temporal outcomes of God's providence when they behave wisely; "If you are wise your wisdom will reward you, if you are a mocker, you alone will suffer" (Proverbs 10:12, NIV). But we must also help teens understand that such positive outcomes are only the tip of the iceberg of what God has in store for them. Faith in Christ—becoming one of his children and being adopted into his family—assures one that, "He who did not spare his own Son but gave him up for us all [those who have faith in Christ], how will he not also with him graciously give us all things?" (Romans 8:32), and that "No eye has seen, no ear has heard, no mind has conceived what God has prepared for those who love him" (1 Corinthians 2:9).

As our teens see good fruit from their decisions, they will naturally be tempted to place their trust in their own ability to produce this fruit. But let us help them raise their vision higher. Let us help them see that it is God who stands behind every material and spiritual blessing. Let us show them from Scripture that while God's ways do produce temporal benefits, we must all look beyond those benefits to the One who offers us the greatest benefit and the only benefit ultimately worth having: himself, in the person of his crucified and resurrected Son.

The Neglect of Repentance

By itself, LCLP is a short-sighted approach to helping angry and unmotivated teens change. Repentance for sin is absolutely necessary for the power of the cross to be unleashed in a young person's life. Earlier on, I made the point that it is not always necessary or wise to point out our teen's sins as they occur. I emphasized that there is more to our teens than their angry, sinful responses. I also said, however, that this does not mean sin can be left unaddressed indefinitely. Wise timing is the key. With angry teens, the most fruitful time to speak to them about their sin is after the bridge is built, not before.

Only the Holy Spirit can lead a young person to true repentance, grief over his sin, and willingness to change. No parent or counselor can produce these responses. But our invitation to the young person to call his sin "sin" and to turn from it needs to be part of our counsel, as the Lord gives us access to the young person's heart. There may be times when this is necessary even when we do not have such access. But, out of love, we must draw our teen's attention to the fact that God commands repentance from sinful behaviors and attitudes.

Repentance, of course, is more than making an apology in order to improve a relationship. True repentance is toward God. It will often include confession to other people, but it is principally an acknowledgement and commitment to turn from ways that have been offensive to God, as well as to another person. David's acknowledgement in Psalm 51 was that his sin was principally and ultimately only against one: God. "Against you, you only, have I sinned and done what is evil in your sight" (Psalm 51:4). As the psalm makes clear, he had also sinned against Uriah and Bathsheba. But in view of the fact that what he did was first and foremost a violation of God's commands, it was primarily sin against him.

Our effort must be, as the Lord gives us an entrée to the teen's heart, to lead him to repentance and faith in Christ. Only in this way will our teen find forgiveness and gain access to the divine power that makes lasting, heart-oriented change possible.

The Hope of the LCLP Approach

The fact that there are weaknesses and potential snares in the LCLP approach ought not to surprise or concern us. The larger issue is whether these principles are truly grounded in Scripture and therefore trustworthy. As I have sought to demonstrate in this book, I believe they are biblically grounded, and I have seen time and again how their application can build a bridge to an angry teen where everything else has failed.

The snares inherent in this approach come as a result of not applying scriptural principles consistently or thoroughly. Certainly, even the gospel itself can be compromised in the absence of theological clarity or wise application. Are not most of the New Testament epistles written to believers who had gotten some aspect of the gospel wrong, and as a result were misapplying it? Make no mistake, I am not intending in any way to place the LCLP principles on a level with the gospel. Rather, my point is that a possibility of misunderstanding and misapplication is no reason to resist some truth of Scripture, whether it be "The tongue of the wise commends knowledge," or "Christ died for your sins."

The LCLP features of communication with our teens have to be applied by imperfect people in an imperfect world toward a somewhat uncertain outcome. The absence of absolute certainty of results should not cause us to hesitate to use them, or to use them only sparingly. Our task is to be faithful in what and how we communicate to our teens, always remembering that the ultimate goal of our counsel is to point our teens to the cross and pray that, by God's grace, they choose to go there.

The Hope of the Cross

As you struggle to build the bridge of communication and then work with your teen to help him or her make wise choices, let the presence of Christ, because of the cross, be your joy. As David declared about God's people, "you make him glad with the joy of your presence" (Psalm 21:6). Even during those times when your heart is breaking for your self-destructive teen, the promise of God's presence guarantees his mercy to you, his security and love around you, and the fruit of the Spirit within you. This is the same promise of richness God makes to your young adult.

We must hold out the wonderful, rich, sturdy, robust cross to our unbelieving or believing teen. If he or she has seen any fruitfulness from making wise choices, ask why it seems these good things have happened. The answer, of course, is because of God's goodness. It's the way he's made life to work.

The cross holds out to each living person the offer of reconciliation with God and the possibility of forgiveness of sins. This offer, this possibility, is the only thing that secures for this world the presence of God's mercy and the availability of any goodness whatsoever. The cross makes God's mercy possible. Without it, man's fallen nature would completely dominate every aspect of life. Sin, hopelessness, futility, selfishness, brutality, exploitation, and oppression toward each other would be the only forces at work among us, and we would quickly destroy ourselves. Countless atrocities throughout human history testify plainly to what we are by nature. But the cross both preserves this fallen world from utter disaster and stands as a promise of the perfect reconciliation that is available to each and every individual. Because of what Christ accomplished there, the cross is the promise of salvation for all who trust in him—including your angry teen.

A bridge has value only because it provides passage from one point to another. The relative value of the bridge derives from two things: Its safety as a means of passage, and the desirability of the destination to which it leads. There is no point in building a strong and beautiful bridge to a trackless wasteland. There is no point in building a structurally unsound bridge to an ideal destination. It only makes sense if you have a good, strong bridge to a place worth going to.

Throughout this book we have spoken of the LCLP approach as a bridge of communication to your teen. But we have also made clear that crossing the bridge is not the final goal. When your teen is ready to make a journey of his own, you must point him toward the Son of God, who paid the price to redeem the whole life of those who trust him.

LCLP is the bridge *to* your teen. But the ultimate destination *for* your teen is the cross. Who can sanely turn down the offer of such kindness in the cross?

NOTES

1. *The Cosby Show.* Season 8, Episode 1,
Part 1: http://www.youtube.com/watch?v=17GCCwVDdDA&feature=channel
Part 2: http://www.youtube.com/watch?v=QrRUXsDumrM&feature=channel

2. *Age of Opportunity: A Biblical Guide to Parenting Teens.* Paul David Tripp. Philippsburg, NJ: P&R Publishing. 1997, 189.

3. *The Peacemaker: A Biblical Guide to Resolving Personal Conflict.* Third Edition. Ken Sande. Grand Rapids, Michigan: Baker Books. 2006.

4. *The Book of Proverbs, Volume II.* Bruce K. Waltke. Grand Rapids: Wm. B. Eerdmans Publishing Company. 2005, 131.

SCRIPTURE INDEX

HELPFUL REMINDERS

Listen Big for not wants
Clarify Narrow for wise wants
Look Wide for exceptions
Plan Small for realistic and hopeful changes

PART I: STANCE

1. Seek first God's glory
2. Check your own heart motives
3. Identify the log in your own eye first
4. Reference your own sins and failures

PART II: LCLP

Listen Big

Five Pylons

1. Listen by echoing your teen's feelings with "quatements"
2. Listen for what your teen does not want
3. Listen to your teen's body language, and listen with your own (R.E.S.O.L.V.E.)
4. Listen to affirm, not necessarily to agree
5. Listen until you see the paradoxes

Clarify Narrow

Five Realities

1. *Wise Wants*-good desires that God has hardwired into teens
2. *The Power of Choosing*-teens have the ability to make real choices
3. *The Pain of Choosing Poorly*- foolish choices yield painful consequences
4. *The Question of Control*- there are things the teen can and cannot control
5. *Relationship with Christ*-speak about this after bridge is built, not before.

Look Wide

- Use teen's past experiences as exceptions
- Blame him for making wise choices in the past.
- Affirm you teen's "freedom" and "control" to change or not change
- Affirm everyone's "lack" of ability to change others
- Hypothesize about possibilities for wise choices and for change
- Hypothesize about the outcomes of non-change
- Note the spiritual resources for enduring change

Plan Small

- Reason about what will happen with and without change
- Plan specific changes
- Convert negative goals to positive ones
- Identify a way to measure change

PART III: MAKING CHANGE STICK

Keep the conversation going

Plan a follow-up conversation

Use open-ended questions and "quatements"

Keep the cross in view

Nudge your teen toward heart concerns